Selling to the Giants

How to Become
a Key Supplier
to Large Corporations

Jeffrey P. Davidson, CMC, MBA
George-Anne Fay

LIBERTY HALL
PRESS™

LIBERTY HALL PRESS books are published by LIBERTY HALL PRESS an imprint of McGraw-Hill, Inc. Its trademark, consisting of the words "LIBERTY HALL PRESS" and the portrayal of Benjamin Franklin, is registered in the United States Patent and Trademark Office.

FIRST EDITION
FIRST PRINTING

© 1991 by Jeffrey P. Davidson
Published by LIBERTY HALL PRESS, an imprint of McGraw-Hill, Inc.

Library of Congress Cataloging-in-Publication Data

Davidson, Jeffrey P.
Selling to the giants : how to become a key supplier to large corporations / by Jeffrey P. Davidson
p. cm.
Includes index.
ISBN 0-8306-7586-8 (h) ISBN 0-8306-3586-6 (p)
1. Industrial marketing. 2. Selling—Industrial equipment.
3. Industrial procurement. 4. Purchasing departments. I. Title.
HF5415.1263.D38 1991   90-21643
658.8—dc20   CIP

For information about other McGraw-Hill materials,
call 1-800-2-MCGRAW in the U.S. In other countries
call your nearest McGraw-Hill office.

Questions regarding the content of this book should be addressed to:
Reader Inquiry Branch
LIBERTY HALL PRESS
Blue Ridge Summit, PA 17294-0850

Vice President and Editorial Director: David J. Conti
Technical Editor: Lori Flaherty
Production: Katherine G. Brown
Book Design: Jaclyn J. Boone

Contents

*To Valerie Anne Davidson, happiness,
long life and best sellers.*

Acknowledgments

IN RANDOM ORDER, WE WOULD LIKE TO ACKNOWLEDGE JIM MORGAN, Harry Houghs, Victor Morris, Leslie Rhatican, Donald Huffmire, Ph.D., Dianne Walbrecker, Bill Holleran, Joe Jeff Goldblatt, Ralph Sharer, Joe Stumpf, David Sandler, Jim Cathcart, Dave Yoho, Alan Cimbergh, J.R. Kimble, Theresa Jensen, Harry Olson, Ph.D., Chester Karrass, Ph.D., Patricia Fripp, D.W. Burke, Philip Kotler, Ph.D., Neil Rackham, Jeff Stevens, and Joanne Tritsch for their information or assistance in helping us complete this book.

Also, thanks to Susan Davidson for her steadfast support, David Conti for acquiring and overseeing development of the manuscript, and all the fine folks at Liberty Hall Press for their professionalism, enthusiasm, and continuing support.

Introduction

ONLY ONE PERCENT OF ALL SMALL BUSINESSES CURRENTLY SELL TO THE nation's largest corporations. This is astounding—and unfortunate, because several million entrepreneurs offer products and services that corporate America needs. What these entrepreneurs lack, and what this book addresses, is a *system* for successfully marketing to major corporations.

If you own or operate your own business and would like to sell to companies larger than you currently serve, this book is for you. In it, we will explore the answers to such questions as:

- What are corporations looking for?
- Where can I find low-cost marketing research information?
- Who do I call on in corporations?
- What are they expecting of me?

While much of marketing is intuitive, corporate marketing is not so clear-cut. When marketing to large corporations, there are rules and protocols that must be honored. You have to be able to talk the language of the corporate purchasing agent, make contact calls, and follow up in a manner that is comfortable for her or him.

This book provides you with step-by-step, detailed information on how to successfully sell your products or services to larger corporations. Before completing this book, I managed a project that involved surveying more than 100 *Fortune 500* purchasing agents, visiting 10 purchasing agents on-site, reviewing successful, corporate-sponsored small business procurement programs, and examining the marketing techniques successful small vendors use in the corporate market. This book contains no theory, no models, no conjecture. The information and advice is based on proven techniques and comes directly from corporate purchasing agents themselves, successful small business vendors, and marketing specialists.

For the now nearly 19 million small businesses in the United States that already market to major corporations but want to improve their techniques, firms that would like to venture forth but haven't done so, and firms that don't even realize that their products or services might be of interest to large corporations, *Selling to the Giants* is a valuable tool.

In chapter 1, we'll look at why quality is a burning issue for corporate purchasers and how you can better position yourself for success in the corporate marketplace. In chapter 2, we discuss what corporations look for, the type of support they offer small suppliers, and why, no matter when and where you start, you can become an insider in this market.

In chapter 3, we examine the need for a business and marketing plan and how to make yourself readily accessible to corporate purchasing agents. The easier they can find you, the easier your marketing task is. In chapter 4, we focus on the fundamentals of selling, including learning the buyer's language, handling objections, and closing the sale. We also examine how supersellers sell— how do some sales representatives earn $200,000 to $400,000 annually in commissions by calling on corporate accounts?

Chapter 5 walks you through the 13 items that make for effective documentation. You'll also learn how to prepare a brochure and other supporting literature. In chapter 6, you'll learn simple methods for breaking through the corporate maze, quickly gathering your own research data, and getting corporations to give you information on how they want to be approached by small vendors.

Chapter 7 provides a detailed job description of key personnel within a corporate purchasing department, including the purchasing manager, purchasing agents, and buyers. Chapter 8 covers the five Ps for being successful: preparation, professionalism, presentation, proof, and performance. It also offers techniques on making contact with technical personnel and discovering new needs.

Chapter 9 provides an insiders look at one of the key arenas in which corporate business is conducted—the trade show. You'll learn how to be successful at either exhibiting or merely attending selected trade shows. Chapter 10 covers some of the fine points of providing your product or service in a method that will make the purchaser notice your firm as not just another supplier.

Chapter 11 covers a potpourri of financing, negotiating, and contacting maneuvers that can keep your firm on even footing and enable you to avoid so many of the pitfalls that snare other small suppliers. It also contains a valuable resource of key insights to selling to corporate giants.

New technology is opening up global markets for even the smallest of suppliers. The 1990s will, undoubtedly, be a time of unprecedented change. Change that can mean substantial opportunity and growth for your company. The corporate marketplace can provide your firm with substantial revenues and security. If you are willing to take the necessary steps to be successful in selling to corporate purchasing agents, then the coming decade can be a spectacular one for your business.

1

Attaining key supplier status

WHETHER YOU ARE NEW TO THE CORPORATE MARKET ARENA OR A veteran, you must recognize that the nature of relationships between large corporations and their key suppliers is rapidly changing. If you want to sell to corporate giants, you'll be asked to provide a variety of functions that were previously handled by the corporate purchasing department themselves.

What is the nature of these changing relationships, and what separates winning suppliers of large corporations from the also-rans? It is a combination of many things. Foremost, however, is that both buyers and sellers recognize that developing and maintaining a long-term relationship is essential, particularly if the corporation is a significant customer of the supplier. Many buyers ensure that their accounting departments pay in strict accordance with initiated terms, for example, so that the small supplier is paid promptly. With a healthy cash flow, the supplier can continue to effectively serve the corporate buyer. It is no wonder then that the ninetys will see increased cooperation and participation between corporate purchasing departments and key suppliers to ensure their mutual prosperity.

If you expertly produce any one of a number of durable goods or provide any one of a number of services, then Xerox, Raytheon, and General Motors, to name a few of several thousand corporate giants will be happy to hear from you. But be forewarned: world-wide competition has prompted all corporate giants to seek the best possible sources of service and supply. Corporate giants today are more inclined to do business with qualified suppliers from around the world, if that's what it takes to get the price, quality, delivery, and other terms they need to be purchase successfully.

Given the choice, most American corporations would prefer to do business with domestic suppliers, the closer the buy, the better. This is true because there many, many hidden cost of using overseas suppliers, among them are the cost of:

- Identifying potential suppliers
- Certifying suppliers to be used
- Tooling and machining to make parts
- Agent commissions, brokerage fees, other middleman expenses
- Warehousing
- Shipping, insurance, and inventory costs
- Export fees, documentation, extra paperwork
- Shipping, unloading, freight, delivery
- Customs fees, import fees, duties, and surcharges
- Foreign exchange rates

Despite these additional costs, many domestic corporations are still forced to go beyond U.S. borders to find qualified suppliers because not enough domestic suppliers ascribe to the levels of quality that large corporations seek. One buyer noted that, "the supplier base in this country has a long way to go to understand the Japanese level of quality." A purchasing VP at another company commented, "all things being equal, we would prefer to source domestically. It is a matter of convenience, language, and culture. But all things are not equal, and we have to find the best available sources if we are to remain successful."

Too many suppliers quote a delivery date and even confirm the date but never call once to say that there is a problem in their production schedule and that actual delivery might be 15, 30, or 45 days after the target date.

One purchasing manager lamented, "We don't seem to be able to train suppliers to call us first." The situation occurs when suppliers over-promise in their deal to close a sale. Corporate purchasing departments have seen this happen time and time again and don't enjoy being taken advantage of. Some suppliers get stuck because they don't have sufficient inventory on hand to meet their promised delivery dates while others simply lack sufficient internal planning to deliver as promised.

Although developing and cementing vendor/large corporation partnerships is a desirable development for everyone, corporate trust and confidence in suppliers often breaks down because purchasing departments often find out about late shipments only when the goods don't arrive as scheduled. Many buyers spend an inordinate amount of time on the phone trying to run down what happened to a shipment and when it will be arriving, forcing them to commit additional dollars on warehousing and excessive inventory to compensate for slow deliveries.

The quality factor

In addition to meeting delivery dates on a timely basis, the quality of goods and services is a sore spot. In one survey of its readers, *Purchasing Magazine* found that an average of 92 percent of goods met the quality specifications as contracted for. In other words, 8 percent of goods—two in every 25—did not meet quality standards. This is a serious blow for the corporate buyer and a quick ticket to a loss of contracts for suppliers. "Too many of our suppliers are complacent about quality," says one purchasing manager. "They talk about improving quality but it is not reflected in the goods we receive."

Today, corporate buyers need a great deal of information before choosing a company for a prime supplier. Competition is keener than ever and large companies are forced to rely more heavily on efficient, dependable vendors (see chapter 5). Corporate purchasing agents are expecting more from their suppliers, particularly in the area of quality. Some large companies estimate that they acquire 70 percent of their quality problems from vendor's shipments; the vast majority of end product quality headaches are shipped into their plants by suppliers in the form of sub-par goods and materials. One purchasing agent observed, "there is no way we can improve the quality of what we are doing without improvements in incoming components."

The good news is that, if you are able to guarantee shipments, you have a distinct advantage over those who do not or cannot.

Achieving favored supplier status

The Xerox Corporation, regarded as having premier purchasing programs, undertook a "drastic pruning" of its supplier base while providing intensive training to key suppliers in statistical process control and just-in-time inventory systems. Xerox has also helped suppliers with personal development programs and long-term contracts that compel suppliers "to become business partners, and build confidence to the point where suppliers share what they have learned."

Among industrial corporations, the average number of suppliers is declining, while single sourcing (finding a source of supply for a particular item or service) is growing in popularity. More than ever, observes one veteran, relationships are up for grabs. "Even long standing personal relationships are at risk." Some purchasers are limiting the number of sales representatives who call on them.

When a corporate giant makes the decision to reduce their supplier base it enables them to maintain more direct and effective communications with remaining suppliers. It also increases corporate leverage over suppliers, because each supplier does more business with the corporate giant and thus is more dependent upon the corporate giant. The net result is clear. If you want to achieve favored vendor or supplier status among corporations who have been tearing down their supplier base, you will have to understand and serve their needs more than ever before, and position your company to become the type of supplier purchasing agents want to call upon.

Learning the rules

To be a successful key supplier, you need to understand the components of supplier/buyer relationships.

Vendor contributions to value analysis

Vendors who have been particularly successful in winning long-term contracts with major corporations make key contributions to value analysis. So, what is value analysis? It is the continual researching, refinement, and adaptation of products so that they can be built faster, less expensively, more durably, or be improved in some other significant way.

The supplier who is able to assist the corporate purchasing agent in meeting the agent's buying needs and helping to increase value analysis becomes a valued, if not highly favored, supplier. Corporations seek supplier input. After all, who else is in a better position to suggest new and improved approaches to manufacturing the goods that they supply?

The supplier's success in contributing to a vendor's value analysis becomes a key marketing tool. Any improvement a supplier is able to suggest or implement suggests he is continuously on the look-out for cost saving, product-enhancing changes. In addition, the supplier can emphasize his role in contributing to value analysis in one corporation when marketing to another corporation. Value analysis becomes a tool for indicating a supplier's "innovativeness" and extensive concern for the buyers welfare.

Supplier supply and quality control

In the 1990s, suppliers will be called upon more often to provide quality control for parts and supplies that they produce and deliver. When the supplier can guarantee an agreed upon level of quality, major industrial buyers are freed from this function. This reduces buyers through-put time in producing the final product. Supplier-based quality control also reduces a corporation's labor, inventory, and returned shipment costs. Vendor-supplied Quality Control is a natural evolution of the supplier/buyer relationship, a phenomenon that will grow in popularity throughout the 1990s.

Once a working relationship is established in which the supplier will supply quality control, and this program proves to be successful, the corporate purchasing department gains tremendous confidence and trust in the supplier.

Servicing national accounts

A survey of more than 1,000 office product buyers and their managers conducted by *Purchasing Magazine* revealed that at least 60 percent of respondents already had ongoing national accounts programs. Companies such as Deere and Company now rely upon teams of factory buyers who meet on a regular basis to develop collective product sourcing strategies for commonly used or commodity goods such as bearings, fasteners, tires, steel, belts, hoses, and so forth.

Many purchasing divisions are turning towards national accounts to take care of commodity goods, particularly in the area of office supplies from items such as copiers, typewriters, telecommunications equipment, personal computers, desktop publishing equipment, image/graphic equipment, electronic data interchanges, systems furniture, and forms management. Some corporate purchasing offices are turning towards blanket agreements with suppliers whereby one supplier has responsibility for all of a particular type of good; systems contracting—whereby a supplier supplies a complete system including all interface or peripheral accessory parts; and stockless inventory, whereby suppliers provide quality control, warehousing, and just-in-time delivery services.

Life-of-the-program contracts

Suppliers who prove themselves by contributing to value analysis, assuming responsibility for the quality control function, or who indicate superior performance in terms of traditional measures such as price, quality, and delivery, are often invited to participate in life program contracts. A life-of-the-program contract essentially guarantees that a vendor will be called upon to supply a particular product or service for as long as the customer, generally a major corporation, has a prime contract.

For example, if an aerospace manufacturer wins a multi-year contract with the Department of Defense to design and produce an advance air surveillance system, than a vendor supplying equipment in support of such a system would retain that status for the duration of the prime contractor's contract.

Suppliers who have successfully served in life-of-the-program contracts are also able to leverage such relationships with one corporation while seeking to obtain life of the program contracts in other corporations. The obvious benefits to the supplier are larger, longer-term contracts with predictable cash flows and predictable revenues, all of which enable the supplier to build a sound business by having fewer but more valuable contracts.

The corporate buyer benefits also. Corporations who know they have a supplier in whom they can rely on are able to meet their program goals and timetables with more regularity and are able to maintain greater project cost control on a long-term basis.

Corporate-sponsored, supplier training programs

After corporate purchasing departments have had a successful experience with a supplier, or when the supplier has established himself in some unique way, some corporations are willing to pay for supplier training. This training serves many functions. For one, if a supplier is close to being qualified to providing a particular product or service but not quite there, then the training can help close the gap. Thus, the supplier adds to his proficiency while the corporation gains another key source of supply.

In addition, the supplier is able to learn more about the corporate customer and is better able to serve. The corporation assists the supplier in becoming more cost conscious and more efficient, positioning itself for long-term cost savings. Finally, both parties establish stronger personal relationships as most of the supplier training is usually on site at corporate headquarters or key branches.

While supplier contributions to value analysis, quality control, life-of-the-contract programs, and corporate sponsorship of supplier training programs, seem to be advanced elements of supplier corporate relationships, winning suppliers actually seek and nurture these program elements as a normal course of doing business.

Keys to success

There are many ways vendors position themselves for success in serving the corporate marketplace, including:

Defining a service strategy   Successful suppliers encapsulate their philosophy of customer service. Usually, this need not be more than a 100- or 150-word description that conveys a promise to the customer and states how the company will stand by its word. This service statement is often made part of the company's literature. Segments of it might also appear on company vehicles, letterhead, and so forth.

Handling special requests   Successful suppliers regard special requests as opportunities for establishing themselves as companies of distinction. A late-night delivery, or any sudden request is viewed as a challenge rather than a burden.

Serving as consultants   Large industrial buyers often look to the supplier or seller as a consultant who can counsel them regarding particular purchase decisions.

Maintaining reserve and replacement parts   Successful suppliers recognize that, in addition to meeting contract specifications, they will also be looked upon as the source for "spare parts" to products or service equipment they are supplying.

Developing instruction and spec sheets   Plain English, easy-to-follow instructions enhance a supplier's status. These can be supplied for everything from how to properly unpackage delivered goods to properly treating or getting the most use out of them. Even on routine shipments, winning suppliers know that the personnel receiving such shipments might be new or unfamiliar with the product or part. Every transaction and every shipment is treated as if it were the first.

Developing internal standards   While the customer might only require A, B, and C, the supplier positioned for long-term success often supplies A, B, C, and D, or A, B, C, D, and E. This might not be possible for all products, all deliveries, or all contracts, but offering that extra touch is a marketing masterstroke when the buyer knows it is being done and acknowledges its value in his operations.

Surveying the corporate customer   An innovative, powerful tool for ensuring that a contract is being fulfilled correctly, is to survey the customer, no matter how large they are. Successful suppliers boldly query corporate receiving dock managers, shipping clerks, engineers, buyers, field representatives, and others to make sure that the supplier is serving the needs of the corporation across-the-board.

Offering regular, positive reports and update   Some suppliers who handle contracts where work is performed for customers over an extended period of time supply weekly or monthly progress reports. These reports can be used as tools for effective position marketing. They are more than a recanting of the performance and effort of the supplier; they are an opportunity to re-affirm the buyer's choice in contracting with the supplier in the first place and to bolster his/her feelings about using the supplier again.

Standing in their shoes

Purchasing World surveyed its readers to determine the major problems they face. A host of wide-ranging concerns included:

- Finding better ways to get things accomplished to meet worldwide competition.
- Keeping lead times short, quality high, and unit prices down.
- Reducing paperwork and paper shuffling.
- Obtaining favorable, long-term price commitments.
- Determining actual costs of freight before shipping.
- Finding the proper balance between price, quality, and the desire for long-term supplier relations.
- Getting quality material at a competitive price as scheduled.
- Balancing incoming sales against forecasted production.
- Coping with seasonal product lines.
- Maintaining good communications with engineering, maintenance, and production personnel.
- Anticipating needs and lead times.

- Reducing production parts and operating supplies to achieve minimum inventories.
- Identifying, evaluating, and breaking in new vendors/suppliers.
- Expediting crucial orders.
- Orienting supplies to just-in-time systems.
- Handling too many shipments where suppliers have not conformed to requirements.
- Maintaining a fully competitive purchasing cycle throughout a product's life cycle.
- Determining actual needs versus initial design estimates.
- Coping with price fluctuations with long-term contracts.

If your goal is to successfully serve as a key supplier to corporate giants, your mission is clear: make the purchasing agents job easier!

2

Finding a
profitable niche

UNFORTUNATELY, MANY SUPPLIERS, INCLUDING MANUFACTURERS, BUT
particularly nonmanufacturers such as construction contractors
and professional service providers who could successfully serve as
key suppliers to corporate giants, don't recognize the varied marketing opportunities available.

Too many suppliers, when considering their marketing potential with a particular corporation, focus only on that company's
end product. "If Corporation X makes widgets, they must want
only widget parts." This narrow focus can lead the contractor or
professional service provider to believe that he or she has nothing
to offer that corporation.

For example, at Polaroid, there is a need for service vendors in
such diverse areas as transportation, construction, data entry, and
even snow removal. Polaroid also seeks suppliers of office furniture, electronic equipment, chemicals, and fuels. Chesebrough-
Pond's uses diverse vendors, from a manufacturer of hoses and
gaskets to a pharmaceutical laboratory.

After making initial contact with the purchasing office and
being careful to "work through the system," which is explained in

chapter 8, you can call on the key technical people who might need specialized professional or contractor services.

Don't be put off because one office, department, or purchasing agent within a corporation says, "We can't use your product or service," or is otherwise discouraging. Your product or service might be in great demand elsewhere in the corporation.

Discovering what corporations need

What, then, are some of the wide-ranging needs of major corporations? The following list includes just some of the opportunity areas:

Accounting Services—Corporate purchasing directors will tell you that there are numerous professional service opportunities throughout their corporations, chief among these are accounting services.

Advertising—Large corporations traditionally spend millions of dollars each year promoting their various products and employ a wide variety of services in advertising and public relations.

Architecture—Continuous additions, renovations, and remodeling of internal and external corporate facilities create the opportunity to provide architectural services.

Audiovisual Production—Corporations often require audiovisual services, but not often enough to have in-house capability. Consequently, opportunities are available in this field.

Bar Coding—From spare parts and office supplies to finished end products, large companies are using bar coding devices to catalog and control assets.

Building Management—Building management includes services such as energy audits, emergency equipment, and maintenance.

Clipping Services—Large corporations are always interested in reviewing how they are portrayed in the print media and might need to concentrate on specific geographic areas.

Computer Software—Corporate data processing departments often need custom-designed software for specialized applications.

Construction—Most corporations are continuously in the process of constructing roadways, parking lots, or new buildings. Many corporations have massive construction projects underway that require the use of small contractors.

Note: The Business Development Committee of the Associated Builders and Contractors in conjunction with the University of Washington is just completing a study of the construction needs and practices of the Fortune 1000 firms with special emphasis on contractor selection criteria and procedures. For further information, contact the director of industry relations, (202) 637-8800 at AB&C.

Data Processing—Data entry and conversion are best handled by firms that specialize in this service to reduce the error rate and startup time to "learn the system" by in-house staff.

Demolition/Disposal—The demolition/disposal needs of major corporations can rival that of any municipality or city-based developer.

Electrical Contracting—As more computers, terminals, and peripherals invade the workplace, the need for rewiring and restructuring existing facilities increases. In addition, electrical contractors are needed whenever a company renovates, redesigns or adds to its facilities.

Electronic Data Interchanges—Modems, jacks, couplers, links, and all forms of interchanges are in great demand.

Engineering Services—All types of engineering (civil, mechanical, chemical, biochemical, stress analysis, and structural) can be used by corporations in the development state for new products or in the design stage of new structures.

Environmental Services—The impact of corporate operations on the environment is a hot issue. Specific expertise in various aspects of environmental protection and impact analysis are of interest to nearly all corporations.

Food Services—Large corporations feed tens of thousands of employees each day.

Graphics—To achieve a fresh approach in graphic design, firms often seek new sources of talent. A major corporate account would be a real asset in a business' marketing portfolio.

Health Services Planning—Some corporations seek health service planners and programs to assist with corporate human resource development.

Industrial Design/Exhibit—The marketing divisions of major corporations frequently send staff to trade shows and exhibits. Imaginative and creative exhibits are always in demand.

Landscaping—Corporations need landscape contracting services for the same reasons that commercial developers and government agencies need them—to maintain the facility's appearance.

Legal Services—As society grows more complex, a wider variety of legal services are needed by corporations, some of which might not be provided by their legal departments.

Management Consulting—All of the top 1,000 corporations in the United States have employed the services of one or more consultants in the past 12 months. Consulting engagements range from feasibility studies to placement services.

Noise Impact Studies—Noise impact, particularly within the office, is another area offering potential opportunities.

Office Furniture and Supplies—Desks, lamps, tables, computer furniture, fixtures, dividers, cabinets, shelves, chairs; plus pens, paper, etc.

Peripheral Equipment—Add-on enhancements to existing equipment are welcome when a supplier can demonstrate increased productivity or reduced costs.

Protective Equipment and Garments—The Occupational Safety and Hazard Administration, or OSHA, has tightened the screws requiring personal protective equipment for laborers in the manufacturing plant.

Recycling—All types of recycling equipment and services is becoming increasingly of interest to corporate purchasing agents.

Research—Depending upon the type of research and/or testing provided, there can be many opportunities within different product lines of the same corporation.

Repair Services—While much of the equipment and machinery used by corporations is under warranties or service contracts, general repair services are always in demand.

Security—Major corporations, particularly their CEOs and presidents, recognize the growing need for corporate and personal security, and they want reliable services and systems.

Storage—Many plant sites with fixed plant capacity and storage availability must seek nearby facilities to relieve the need for heavy plant-related expenditures.

Systems Furniture—Includes all forms of integrated work stations for EDP users.

Temporary Help—Hiring temporary professional staff to smooth out work cycles while otherwise keeping total payroll at an acceptable minimum has caught on among corporate giants. Part-time lawyers, accountants, engineers, as well as word processors, trainers, and others, can now be found in many corporate headquarters and are increasingly procured by corporate purchasing departments!

Transportation—Most corporations need trucking companies to deliver their supplies and transport their products to the marketplace. For its own fleet of vehicles, a corporation will need equipment and maintenance, security and protection services, and mobile communication equipment and services.

Videotape Production—Videotape production is especially needed by human resource departments for in-house training programs.

Waste Disposal Service—Corporate waste disposal sites are near capacity and alternatives to existing waste disposal sites are welcome.

Waste disposal services is one of the fastest-growing service needs for corporations. Newspaper and magazine headlines about the greenhouse effect during the last several years have strongly impacted corporations, particularly within purchasing departments. Tales of illegal dumps, midnight runs, and "let's bury it and forget it" are giving way to higher measures of corporate responsibility.

The Dupont Corporation, for example, diligently examines the backgrounds and facilities of firms claiming that they specialize in toxic waste disposal and treatment. The prevailing view among corporations today is that the disposal of hazardous wastes must be followed through to its conclusion. Some corporations, such as Union Carbide, seek full-service firms that are able to both treat and dispose of hazardous waste. This enables the corporation to trace all shipments of waste leaving its plants. At both Dupont, Union Carbide, and dozens of other corporate giants, hazardous waste disposal services have become a highly centralized controlled purchase. If you can help in these areas, your company is in demand now more than ever.

Don't assume that a corporate giant cannot use your service just because it might not be directly related to the corporation's end products. Contractors and professional service companies, as well as manufacturers who cannot recognize the wide-ranging opportunities of major corporations, are limiting their potential. It will take some prospecting to identify the right corporate contacts, but the potential rewards certainly justify the effort.

Who are the largest buyers and how much do they annually spend? The top 100 purchasing departments in the U.S. ranked by purchasing expenditures account for some half trillion dollars in expense, equal to 10 percent of all of the purchases in the nation in a given year. See Fig. 2-1.

'89 Rank	'88 Rank	Company	'88 purchasing $ spent (in millions)	% change in $ spent	$ spent as a % of sales	Sales rank
1	1	General Motors	62000	24	56	1
2	2	Ford	54000	25	60	2
3	4	Chrysler	22000	30	65	8
4	5	IBM	19000	26	32	4
5	3	General Electric	18000	0	46	7
6	7	AT&T	9500	5	30	9
7	6	Du Pont	9000	0	30	11
8	8	United Technologies	8320	4	46	26
9	14	Dow Chemical	7340	24	44	32
10	12	McDonnell Douglas	7083	14	47	36
11	9	GTE	7038	1	43	33
12	10	Boeing/Commercial Airplane	6954	10	41	29
13	22	Caterpillar	6700	66	65	61
14	23	Xerox	6564	64	40	34
15	11	Exxon	6417	3	8	3
16	13	Lockheed	6000	0	60	56
17	15	Allied-Signal	5954	7	50	48
18	18	Tenneco	5811	29	37	38
19	16	Goodyear Tire & Rubber	5700	7	53	54
20	21	International Paper	5243	22	55	73
21	27	Union Carbide	5100	37	61	90
22	29	Shell Oil	4965	34	22	13
23	20	Westinghouse Electric	4880	13	39	42
24	17	Mobil	4800	4	9	5
25	19	General Dynamics	4800	11	50	72
26	33	Digital Equipment	4700	51	31	44
27	25	ITT	4616	18	24	79
28	24	Raytheon	4400	11	54	95
29	35	Weyerhaeuser	4001	43	40	66
30	32	3M	3914	25	37	57
31	26	LTV	3762	15	50	56
32	54	USX	3500	58	60	31
33	28	Unisys	3465	2	35	69
34	39	Eastman Kodak	3406	28	20	28
35	30	Rockwell International	3344	-3	28	46
36	31	Emerson Electric	3325	5	50	114
37	47	Textron	3200	31	45	107
38	37	Texas Instruments	3147	16	50	118
39	52	W.R. Grace	3099	37	50	132
40	45	Motorola	3052	22	37	92
41	60	Bethlehem Steel	3005	54	55	148
42	34	Mead	2999	6	67	178
43	66	Deere	2971	59	55	149
44	38	Georgia Pacific	2966	9	31	74
45	41	Martin Marietta	2921	12	51	133
46	100	SmithKline Beckman	2900	168	43	170
47	49	Hoechst Celanese	2839	21	50	137
48	42	Champion International	2820	11	55	157
49	44	PPG Industries	2808	12	50	139
50	36	TRW	2792	2	40	112
51	90	Apple Computer	2700	111	65	180
52	51	Navistar/Int'l. Transp.	2652	15	65	191
53	59	Dana	2595	25	50	155
54	58	Bayer-USA	2568	22	54	169
55	43	N. American Phillips	2500	0	50	143
56	40	Triangle Industries	2462	-5	60	185
57	56	Kimberly-Clark	2437	10	45	151
58	67	Alcoa	2369	30	24	71
59	46	Texaco USA	2348	-4	7	10
60	55	James River	2294	4	45	138
61	62	Honeywell	2240	17	31	110
62	57	Litton Industries	2224	4	45	161
63	82	Paccar	2209	48	71	255
64	69	Cooper Industries	2129	18	50	187
65	73	Chevron	2094	25	8	14
66	65	American Cyanamid	2066	10	45	175
67	80	Eaton	2033	35	48	235
68	77	Dresser Industries	1994	24	50	200
69	85	Reynolds Metals	1985	42	39	145
70	91	Scott Paper	1933	52	41	172
71	74	Combustion Engineering	1916	14	55	233
72	68	Whirlpool	1901	5	43	181
73	75	Hewlett-Packard	1867	15	19	63
74	70	Boise Cascade	1842	7	45	194
75	61	Monsanto Chemical	1800	-5	40	91
76	72	Grumman	1795	6	50	215
77	88	Teledyne	1760	36	40	176
78	76	Amoco	1692	4	8	18
79	83	Stone Container	1684	15	45	212
80	63	National Intergroup	1643	-13	48	268
81	87	American Standard	1635	-25	44	213
82	84	Ingersoll-Rand	1631	14	54	264
83	89	Quantum Chemical	1617	26	50	273
84	71	FMC	1600	-6	50	242
85	-	NCR	1600	14	27	123
86	81	Unocal	1558	3	18	77
87	86	Occidental Petroleum	1553	13	8	21
88	-	Great Northern Paper	1435	38	40	221
89	-	Olin	1419	32	55	335
90	-	Honda USA	1414	12	-	
91	93	Armco	1409	11	43	247
92	78	Atlantic Richfield	1400	-12	8	25
93	97	Air Products & Chemicals	1360	13	56	316
94	92	Owens-Corning Fiberglas	1300	3	55	280
95	-	Control Data	1220	13	34	217
96	94	Northrop	1217	-2	21	131
97	99	Mack Trucks	1200	14	57	365
98	-	Zenith Electronics	1208	13	45	300
99	96	Inland Steel	1200	0	50	197
100	-	Parker Hannifin	1200	68	52	324

Fig. 2-1. The top 100 purchasing organizations.

Small supplier assistance

The question often comes up, "Do corporations help small developing businesses that want to do business with them?" If you are a small domestic supplier who otherwise can meet the challenge of a key supplier to corporate giants, you'll be pleased to learn that many corporations have a strong commitment to using and supporting qualified small suppliers.

About one-third of corporate giants help small, developing businesses in some way. In fact, some companies have a policy specifically for dealing with small, developing companies. Others have established small business supplier offices. Some corporations even produce and distribute directories of suppliers to their purchasing agents at all corporate branches.

Many large corporations have prepackaged information for would-be suppliers on what goods and services are being sought. Corporations are increasingly providing the names and phone numbers of purchasing agents by plant or location.

A few highly progressive companies, such as Control Data and Conoco, provide specialized management, financial, or technical assistance to small, developing businesses. Many corporations also maintain an internal, computerized directory of small business supplier capabilities.

Progressive corporations actually set goals for small developing businesses. The goals are set in the form of dollar, or percentage, of total purchases.

Small business purchasing programs

The development of small business purchasing programs by so many large corporations demonstrates their commitment to take the lead in increasing growth and marketing opportunities for small businesses. To ensure maximum economic return, these small businesses are required to participate in capital formation and productivity.

The activities and programs of major corporations directly affect their respective business communities. Populated by large corporations who are sensitive to contracting with smaller suppliers, many business communities have experienced additional investment opportunities for community residents, new construction and renovation of commercial property, increased purchasing and leasing of initial equipment, increased employment opportunities, and expansion of the local tax base with the resulting reduction of local tax burdens.

Corporate public relations officers also know that using small business suppliers helps to offset negative attitudes the public might have regarding a corporation.

Major corporations that serve as prime contractors to the federal government, such as McDonnell Douglas, Martin Marietta, and Northrop must, by law, submit summaries of their subcontracting activity to the U.S. Small Business Administration.

Commitment and follow-through

The success of any small supplier purchasing program is directly related to the level of commitment and endorsement of the chief executive officer. It is the CEO who makes it clear that this program will (or will not) become an integral part of the normal business operation. To achieve an effective small business purchasing program, however, there must be a coordinated effort throughout the organization. To facilitate this coordination, many giant corporations appoint one individual to develop, guide, and monitor the program.

The coordinator functions primarily as a central information source and contact point for company buyers and small suppliers. The coordinator's duties include identifying potential suppliers and soliciting information from them, conducting seminars and workshops for purchasing personnel and small suppliers, and monitoring the program's performance.

"When dealing with small suppliers, a distinction must be made," points out a purchasing officer with FMC in Chicago, "between qualified and qualifiable." Many potential suppliers are qualifiable and with some assistance, they become qualified. Very few suppliers will initially meet the standard requirements for suppliers (see chapters 5 and 8).

To bring these suppliers up to standards requires efforts beyond normal purchasing department procedures. While most corporations are not prepared to make this effort, some do. The following is a list of a few of the ways that purchasing coordinators in progressive corporations assist small suppliers:

- Provide technical, managerial, and financial assistance.
- Allow longer lead times.
- Arrange special payment terms.
- Broaden product specifications.
- Supply information on pricing practices, bid preparation, production, sales, and servicing.

- Assist in developing a quality control program.
- Has in-house small business supplier policy.
- Maintains a separate small business program office.
- Uses external small business supplier directories.
- Provides information on goods and services purchased.
- Provides names and phone numbers of plant purchasing agents.
- Offers special assistance (management, financial, technical) to small business suppliers.
- Maintains a directory, or file, on small business vendor capabilities.
- Sets dollar or percentage goals for its small business vendor utilization.
- Provides incentives to purchasing staff to use small business suppliers.

Some corporations, such as Todd Shipyards and Honeywell, have established aggressive, small supplier procurement goals. These goals provide a target for expected performance as well as an indicator of actual performance. Corporate goals can be based on:

- percentage of purchase;
- dollar value of contracts;
- number of contracts; and
- number of small vendors used.

Other goals can include the number of visits to vendor sites; the number of new vendors used; and the number of contracts of a given size awarded to small vendors.

Everyone starts as strangers

Now, let's look at a case of an entrepreneur who knew what he had to offer was in demand, but never took the first step because he felt like an outsider.

Matt Richardson, a Decatur, Illinois entrepreneur went to a trade show in Chicago where he saw one of his competitors smiling and joking with the corporate purchasing agent of a firm he wants to sell to. A few days later, he reads a press release in his local newspaper that details how another small firm in the next county was able to grow 23 percent in one year due to its acquisition of several large clients.

Matt's mental receptors are set to see, hear, and receive messages indicating that everyone knows everyone else and efforts to win new business with major corporations would be fruitless because his business is not well known. Matt is not alone. A common myth that seems to pervade small entrepreneurs is that, on an individual level, we each have a deck stacked against us because of the unfair advantage that others maintain over us. But do others really have inside connections that they are able to use for superior marketing results?

Yes and no.

"No" from the standpoint that everyone in this world starts off as a stranger to everyone else. Even your own parents were strangers to you until you got to know them. Looked at from this perspective, we are more easily reminded that people that we know in this world and the connections that we have made are largely results of our own choices and our own actions.

Do some of your competitors maintain an advantage over you because of who they know? Most assuredly. Returning to Matt's situation, the one competitor he saw laughing and joking with a corporate purchasing agent had to have spent time calling on, meeting, and getting to know that purchasing agent. Along the way, luck factors could have certainly played a part in the success of Matt's competitor. In the long run, however, those that are "wired" or have the inside connection usually worked for it by allocating time, energy, and money toward cultivating that key introduction, presentation, and follow-up.

When I was a freshman in high school, the junior varsity soccer coach accepted everyone for the team who showed up at tryout. While in the early weeks of the season we often had many more bodies at practice than we would need during the season, the coach knew that the development of the team was largely a self-selection process. Those who wanted to play stuck it out all the way. The only players that were cut were those who cut themselves—they stopped coming to practice.

Making key connections with corporate purchasing agents is also largely a self-selection process. They can't possibly get to know you if, as Earl Nightengale said, "You're one of the timid feeders in the lagoon who never ventures out into the broad deep sea." And they can't possibly get to know you unless you show up—show up at their plant, show up at trade shows, show up by mailing them appropriate information, and show up by calling.

Peter Drucker, says, "Business has only two basic functions: marketing and innovation." And that great observer of life, Woody

Allen, says, "just showing up is 85 percent of everything." I once attended a regional meeting of the White House Conference on Small Business. In one session, numerous entrepreneurs were commenting on how difficult it was for them to effectively market their firms. This "line" was quite popular among the majority of participants in the room, they too being small business entrepreneurs.

Risking unpopularity for the balance of the session, I posed a question to the group. "How many of you, right now, can tell me the name of at least one purchasing agent from a major corporation?" Everyone in the room was silent. For a long three or four seconds no one said a thing. Risking even greater unpopularity, I said, "then you are going to have a very difficult time ever selling to large firms."

I expected a verbal free-for-all against me. It didn't happen. Surprisingly, the issue was not dealt with at all. The next person to speak brought up another topic. The moderator followed the lead and my crafted gem, which I thought would represent a turning point in the meeting and help participants realize unless they *knew* purchasing agents, they weren't ever going to sell to them, was quickly lost in the scuffle.

If it appears that everybody else maintains competitive advantages fraught with key connections, ask yourself, "Have I cut myself off of the team or will I stick it out and play this season?"

3

Successful marketing strategies

WHEN ASKED, MANY ENTREPRENEURS REPORT THAT THEY WOULD LIKE to have a corporate giant under contract but it would take an inordinate effort to achieve this. "I don't have time to get involved in long-term marketing right now," or "We'll get around to documenting our production system later this year," or "I'd like to call on major corporations but I am not prepared."

The list of excuses is endless. Entrepreneurs report that they don't have enough leads, enough money, or enough time. There are literally millions of suppliers who could serve large companies but who continue to do nothing to further their opportunities or expose themselves to this market. "Marketing is . . . much broader than selling," says Peter Drucker. "It encompasses the entire business . . . seen from the point of its final result, that is, from the customer's point of view."

If you are a seasoned business veteran, you can skim this chapter. Otherwise, information in this chapter might prove to be more valuable to your business than you first suspected.

Creating business and marketing plans

Ideally, the start of a business should commence with a business plan but few entrepreneurs ever produce a complete business plan. A business plan is a document that you produce for yourself that guides you in your thinking. It focuses on marketing, financing, and human resources—all the elements that make your business successful.

Often, the terms *business plan* and *marketing plan* are erroneously used interchangeably. The marketing plan is a subset, or component, of the business plan, the most important subset. If you can't describe what market(s) you will serve, how are you going to generate revenue? Without this, other information in your business plan is meaningless.

Underestimating the effort and time to market to corporate giants are classic mistakes that would-be suppliers repeatedly make. It takes 18 months or more, on the average, to close a contract with a major corporation, from the time you first make contact! Don't lightly dismiss this figure as conjecture or one that is not applicable to you.

If you think the 18-month cycle for marketing to corporate giants is long, it's much worse for marketing new technology. Years ago, author Stephen Rosen published an article in the *New York Times* indicating the time span between the conception of a new product and when it became the marketable product (see Table 3-1). Still, purchasing managers can be very receptive to innovations and technology when you can demonstrate a time or cost savings.

Evaluating your marketing staff

If your company employs more than 12 people, you should probably have at least one full-time marketing person. If you have a small staff and no marketing help, at least 20 to 25 percent of your time should be spent on marketing, and you should delegate marketing support activities such as researching and organizing to someone else. Twenty percent of your time on marketing equals at least 8 hours per week, 400 hours per year, at a *minimum*. Twelve to fifteen hours per week is better, regardless of your other responsibilities.

The easiest way to increase your marketing effectiveness is to free up your time by not handling what can be delegated. Delegating responsibility is unnatural. It is natural to want to do the work

_____Table 3-1._____
Marketing New Technology

Innovation	Conception	Realization	Interval (Yr)
Automatic transmission	1930	1946	16
Ballpoint pen	1938	1945	7
Fluorescent lighting	1901	1934	33
Frozen foods	1908	1923	15
Heart pacemaker	1928	1960	32
Helicopter	1904	1941	37
Long-playing records	1945	1948	3
Minute rice	1931	1949	18
Nylon	1927	1939	12
Photography	1782	1838	56
Radar	1904	1939	35
Radio	1890	1914	24
Roll-on deodorant	1948	1955	7
Silicone	1904	1942	38
Stainless steel	1904	1920	16
Telegraph	1820	1838	18
Transistor	1940	1956	16
Videotape recorder	1950	1956	6
Photocopying	1935	1950	15
Zipper	1883	1913	30

yourself. To find out whether or not you are one of those people who find it difficult to delegate, or who should be delegating more, ask yourself the following questions. These questions were developed by Dr. Donald W. Huffmire, who is an associate professor at the School of Business at the University of Connecticut.

1. Do you frequently take work home?
2. Do you work longer hours than the people you manage?
3. Are your people slow or reluctant to make decisions?
4. Are you frequently interrupted by others coming to you for advice or decisions?
5. Are you doing work that others are paid to do?
6. Do you have trouble meeting deadlines?
7. Do unfinished jobs build up so that you're always "one behind?"
8. Do you spend more time working than planning?
9. Do you lack time to think out future assignments?
10. Are many sudden daily and weekly unexpected emergencies and crises common in your operation?

11. Do you work at details that are low priority to your main objective?

12. Are details your headache because you don't have employees who are capable of handling them?

13. Are simple routine jobs delegated but not promptly done, with much follow-up required?

14. Do you lack confidence in your subordinates abilities?

15. Do you keep details of your job secret from others?

16. Do you feel like you're earning your keep more when you're rushed?

17. Do you feel compelled to keep close tabs on everything that is going on in your operation?

18. Do things get fouled up when you are not on the job?

19. Do you and your subordinates usually not agree on what results are expected from them?

20. Do your people feel that they do not have enough authority to achieve their objectives?

The effective delegator can answer each of these questions with a "No." If you answer "Yes" to even a few of them, you probably are not delegating properly.

As president or manager of a company, it is all too common to want to keep your finger on as many functions as possible. If you have a staff who can handle certain areas of your business, however, you must learn to delegate these tasks. In the long run, your marketing effectiveness will live or die with your ability to delegate.

Huffmire, who has worked with corporations such as Westinghouse and IBM says, "Don't make negative assumptions about your people. If you assume your people don't want more responsibility, don't want to think for themselves, resist change, or must be watched closely, you won't delegate much to them." Instead, you will do more of the work yourself than you should and over control them. The results will be low motivation, low teamwork, low risk-taking, low creative problem-solving, and low marketing effectiveness.

Developing a marketing plan

The purpose of marketing is to plan for your company's long-range future. But it is too easy to do the tasks that bring immediate satisfaction or reward and ignore those that can be put off. This is a natural tendency that must be fought and overcome. If your company is doing reasonably well at the present time, you might forget what it was like when you weren't sure where the next contract was coming from.

Remember, it takes an average of 18 months from an initial contact with a purchasing manager to establish a solid contractual arrangement. At Lever Brothers, for example, they are interested in hearing from new suppliers, but response time in the minds of many suppliers, is very slow. Being slow to respond is commonplace for large corporations.

Plan where you want your company to be in one year, three years, and five years. Include the planning products and services you want to offer, the number of employees, and the amount of space you will need. Make the plans realistic without limiting your growth. Then map out and follow strategies to reach these goals, revising them as necessary. Setting marketing goals will not guarantee success, but evidence strongly supports the theory that goal attainment is far more likely if those goals are clearly identified and serve as a focus.

How one company approaches marketing

One small, but growing firm located in Southern California, whom we'll call CDS, defines itself as being in the business of providing hardware/software system integration and related services to the domestic aerospace and defense industry. CDS maintains a four-pronged approach in its market planning. The following excerpt is from their marketing plan.

CDS possesses key, distinct competitive advantages that enable it to succeed in the marketplace:

1. Its underlying marketing philosophy.
2. The types of individuals employed.
3. The long-term marketing effort undertaken for key opportunities.
4. Superior marketing research capabilities.

1. **Marketing Philosophy**

CDS believes in the full-service approach to serving the needs of industry in the areas of hardware/software integration, communications network analysis and design, systems engineering, systems maintenance, and automated office systems design. The company's existing commitment to maintain hardware and software support for computer systems, for example, spans the continental U.S. CDS has established a strong technical base while maintaining a people-oriented operation.

In the past, 60 percent of CDS's business has been follow-on. Growth or expansion is undertaken only after careful planning, analysis of risk, and assembling of requisite resources. CDS has maintained a reputation for quality and timeliness, and charges a fair price for the value of its products, services, and performance.

This marketing philosophy has essentially enabled CDS to become a $3.5 million plus company, and will serve as the cornerstone for growth. Having developed and maintained an established track record for outstanding performance, CDS enjoys a strong competitive advantage in acquiring new business with existing clients, and in attracting potential new clients through third-party referral; i.e., "word of mouth."

2. **Type of Individual Employed**

CDS employs only top computer service professionals, computer service with proven performance records. CDS matches employees with challenging tasks in familiar environments. These talented individuals have the capability to discuss client problems readily in the client's own terminology, and understand contract requirements literally from both sides of the fence. This capability affords CDS's top management a continuous supply of inside marketing information and marketing opportunities.

CDS project managers provide the level of effort mandated by the contracts to which they adhere, and serve as a network of inside "salespeople" obtaining first-person primary market data for the company in its most lucrative market area.

CDS's strategy in obtaining the right type of contract managers is to identify marketing targets "sole source, noncompetitive in nature," of somewhat modest size which could be used to bring the desired type of individuals on board. CDS is presently bidding on contracts for which these types of individuals can be hired, recognizing the value of their services in the marketing effort required for systems integration.

CDS's staff is supported by excellent working conditions, specialized training when necessary, and a vast array of sophisticated support materials.

3. Long-Term Marketing Effort

CDS's marketing philosophy and the type of individuals employed firmly support the company's third and most important vehicle in achieving a competitive advantage: a long-term marketing effort. Solid marketing intelligence requiring long lead times for tracking is required before any solicitation is made by CDS. Intelligence gathering is a two-way street. The company maintains an active file of all potential projects. Then, once a promising new business target takes shape, CDS calls on its various data sources and prepares a marketing strategy.

Solicitations are generally *not* bid unless they have been tracked over a period of time and a significant amount of intelligence has already been gathered. CDS prefers to know key contacts within corporations and how receptive that corporation would be to a CDS bid.

CDS's marketing intelligence gathering is supported through continuing contact with client representatives; review of industry directories and research reports; membership in trade and professional associations; attendance at pre-bid conferences, marketing seminars, trade shows, and federal government expositions; and leads generated as a result of its five-years in the market place.

CDS's working agreements with original equipment manufacturers, hardware and software firms, and other computer services firms enable CDS to provide competitive products and services.

4. Marketing Research Capabilities

CDS maintains superior marketing research capabilities that enable it to perform in-depth analysis of market opportunities, industry growth and trends, and intensity of competition. CDS also monitors the configuration of other installations at key client locations. All of these capabilities enhances CDS's focus on a potential market opportunity.

Maintaining accessibility

If you are like most suppliers, you'll probably move sometime in the next couple of years. It is a fact of business life. The important thing is to maintain your accessibility to those who would do business with you. Despite the possibility of finding a cost-competitive and highly qualified new supplier, many corporate purchasing managers do not have the time to "beat the bushes," or track your firm down following your relocation.

Consider this scenario. A purchasing agent for Penwalt or Harris is sitting at his desk, considering whom to call for a printed circuit board. He thinks back to the last trade fair he attended and remembers there were four suppliers who might be able to supply the part. He opens a file drawer, ostensively to find the literature they each gave him. Searching through folders, he finds brochures for three out of the four companies.

For two of the numbers he is told, "that phone number has been disconnected." One vendor is left, and that's who gets the appointment.

Whether you have recently moved or have been in the same location since you started in business, it is vital to make it easy for callers to find you. A little effort on your part can make it that much easier for them.

If you move or change your product or service, send an announcement to everyone on your mailing list. Be sure to include a mailing label with the new address with every letter. Also, when *answering* an inquiry by mail, be sure the envelope indicates that the information was requested. Otherwise, it runs the risk of being thrown out during screening. For example, your envelopes could say:

Here Is The Information You Requested!

Mail forwarding

When moving, as soon as you know your new address, get a change of address form from your local post office. Filling out this form will ensure that your mail will be forwarded at no charge for about 12 months. Additionally, your local post office manager has the freedom to extend the duration of the change of address notice. Also, make sure that you list your firm's new or proper address in the directories appropriate to your product or service. These might include:

- service directories
- industry directories
- regional business directories
- local business directories

Rolodex cards

Though more corporate purchasing departments now maintain on-line supplier information, don't overlook the power and simplicity of submitting a Rolodex card to targeted purchasers.

With your initial written contact with a corporation, include a standard size Rolodex card with your name, address, phone, and a few key words describing your product or service. If you have many different types of products, you might want to pick one or two descriptive words that relate to that particular company's needs.

You might want to offer two such cards in each mailing—one for the purchasing agent and one for her assistant. Patricia Fripp, a San Francisco-based corporate and association trainer, uses laminated, preprinted Rolodex cards as her business card and sends two at a time. The tab on one card reads "Fripp, Patricia." The tab on the other cards reads "Speaker." "That way," says Fripp, "if they forget my name, they can still find me." Making it easy for purchasing agents to find you makes it more likely that they will.

Post office boxes

If you anticipate the need to change office and production space due to fluctuations in the volume of business, consider renting a post office box. Sizes are fairly standard across the country. You might find that the disadvantage of picking your mail up at the post office is largely offset by the consistency in your address. This consistency means you will not have to change your business cards or stationery when you move. Be sure to include your street address along with your post office box when possible.

Telephone-responsive

How does your company sound to outsiders? According to super manager Robert Townsend, former head of Avis Rent-A-Car, one way you can easily find out is by phoning in anonymously from time to time and pretending to be a customer who needs help. "You'll find some real horror shows." Worse, try to phone yourself. You'll see clearly says Townsend what "indignities your defenses inflict on callers."

Joe Stumpf, co-owner of Automated Sales Training in North Hollywood, California, managed a project that involved randomly calling 5,000 telephone directory advertisers throughout the United States, each of whom had spent more than $200 per month on their advertisements, to test reactions to phone inquiries.

Each advertiser was asked the following, "I saw your ad in the yellow pages. How much does your product (or service) cost?" The following are the results of this survey as reported by Stumpf (figures add up to more than 100 percent because many firms showed more than one listed reaction).

3,918	(78.4%)	Never asked for our name.
2,791	(55.8%)	Took more than eight rings to answer.
2,117	(42.3%)	Said the price, then, without hesitation, gave us a list of other products or services, but never asked for any action (to buy or make an appointment).
1,711	(34.2%)	Said the price, and, with no further comment, hung up.
573	(11.5%)	Said they didn't know, and asked us to call back when the boss was in.
414	(8.2%)	Put us on hold for more than two minutes.

On the positive side:

42	(0.8%)	Introduced themselves.
77	(1.5%)	Asked us for our phone number.
385	(7.7%)	Said they were the owner of the company.
414	(8.2%)	Had a planned presentation that was professional and made us feel they wanted our business.

These results are amazing and point to a widespread need among all businesses to improve telephone response. Because the first impression of your company might be by phone, it pays to have the phone answered in a professional manner, or not at all! "After seeing these results," Stumpf said, "AST developed 29 telephone techniques for turning phone inquiries into sales, and demonstrated and explained them in an audiotape:

1. Answer the phone on the second or third ring. Your goal when answering the phone is to make the caller feel important and comfortable, and you have about 15 seconds to make a lasting first impression.

2. Never start your phone presentation with an apology. You lose all control and positioning.

3. Answer your phone with enthusiasm, which is contagious and signals a strong commitment to your product and your company.

4. Stand up (if possible) when you answer the phone. It opens the diaphragm and allows your voice to unfold naturally.

5. Smile when you talk. You sound happier.

6. Place a mirror next to your phone. Before you answer, look in the mirror and say, "I answer my phone with enthusiasm."

7. Develop a sincere and positive attitude. People know when you're faking it.

8. Be different. Your competition is probably the ad above or below yours in the yellow pages. Think of creative slogans to use to answer your phone.

9. Speak slowly. The normal rate of speech is 150 words per minute on the phone. Slow down to 100 wpm.

10. Introduce your company, then yourself. Never ask someone their name until you've introduced yourself.

11. Limit your talking—get the other person talking.

12. Have empathy. Listen. Let them know you understand.

13. Don't interrupt. Customers are what keep you in business. Interruptions might turn them off.

14. Take notes. This will help you remember important points.

15. Use interjections. Let the other person know you're still listening.

16. Don't jump to conclusions. Avoid unwarranted prejudgments about customer qualification.

17. Listen for the overtones.

18. Use open-ended questions to gather information about the caller's needs.

19. Use close-ended questions to close a sale or have your customer answer yes or no.

20. Use the porcupine question. Answer a question with a question, to draw information out of your customer.

21. Show the customer that you care. He/she doesn't care how much you know until you show how much you care.

22. Keep the attention on the caller. Eliminate the words "I," "me," and "mine," and replace them with "you" or "we."

23. Use the caller's name—the sweetest sound in the language to him.

24. Be proud of yourself and your position. How you feel about yourself can be heard in your voice.

25. Don't be over anxious to cut your price. On a possible larger order, don't act as if you've never had one.

26. Pause!

27. Use an alternative-choice question when you ask for the order.

28. Never talk about the competition.

29. Show you're grateful and appreciative. Say "Thank you!"

Making your phone number work

Most telephone companies throughout the country will allow you to reserve a special number, as long as it is not in use by another customer. For instance, if you manufacture paint, you could reserve the number 87P-AINT; if you manufacture microchips, you might reserve 27C-HIPS; or if you are a therapist, you could reserve 9AD-VICE. My own phone number, chosen in 1981, is 931-*1984*. My 800 number is 1-800-735-*1994*.

Having a telephone number that makes a marketing point for you will make you more noticeable among competitors, and it makes it easier for the purchasing agent to remember your number without having to look it up. Most telephone companies charge no fee for this service, but check with your local company.

Call forwarding

When you move outside your local area, there are two options regarding your old phone number. You can have your number changed, and the telephone company will offer a recording that gives callers the new number. Because this service is generally free of charge, phone companies will not guarantee how long the recording will stay in place, but most try to keep it on for up to a year. You might also keep your old number when you move and pay an additional service charge each month based on the distance from your original area. Procedures and fees vary so check with the local telephone company.

You work hard to land new contracts. The little extra effort to maintain accessibility ensures that you don't miss an order because purchasing agents can't find you.

4

Mastering selling techniques

REGARDLESS OF THE VALUE OF THE PRODUCT OR SERVICE YOU HAVE TO offer, if you or your marketing staff haven't mastered the fundamentals of selling on a one-to-one basis, your quest to successfully market to the giants will be continually thwarted.

Three keys to successful selling

The three keys to successful selling are: total unshakable belief in yourself; belief in your product; and the ability to close successfully.

1. *Belief in yourself*. You will never be successful in selling until you fully believe in yourself. You might have a superior product or service. You might have many skills in selling. You might be managing or working for a superior organization. You might have hot prospects and a potentially lucrative sales territory. However, you cannot consistently be successful in sales until you firmly and steadfastly believe in yourself.

   Belief in yourself is transmitted to your prospects and clients regardless of what you say or your style of selling.

The prospect first buys "you," before he/she buys your product or service. Entrepreneur and inventor Richard Levy, who has sold dozens of product ideas and inventions to corporate giants, such as Proctor and Gamble, General Foods, and Mattel says, "the first thing that must be sold is yourself. From there the potential for product sales increases." Belief in yourself in selling is so important that without it, the best trained and most professional salesperson may as well seek another profession.

2. *Belief in your product or service.* The second key is belief in your product or service. You must believe strongly that the product or service you are offering represents a sound investment to your prospects. Your product doesn't necessarily have to be the best there is on the market, but you believe it to be the best *value* for the investment. If you drive a Chevy, you can't sell a Ford as effectively as the man or woman who owns a Ford, drives a Ford, and believes in a Ford.

   A salesperson's commitment to his product or service is transmitted to the prospect or client. The enthusiasm you possess for your product or service is contagious. Moreover, it cannot be feigned on a sustained basis. If you are prone to oscillation and don't believe in what you are selling, you can't possibly expect your customers or prospects to do so—and they won't.

3. *Closing skills.* The third key to long-term successful selling is developing effective closing skills. Without the ability to close, your sales presentations will meander hopelessly. The sales that you make will represent a fraction of those that could be made with the use of proper closing techniques.

   What is a closing sentence? It's any question to which the answer confirms that the sale has been made. Some sales professionals are seemingly natural closers; they have no qualms about repeatedly asking for the order. For most of us, however, closing techniques must be learned. Belief in yourself and your product are qualities that are generated from within, closing abilities must be learned.

Developing effective closing skills

Of the three keys to successful selling, closing techniques are probably the most important. Not surprisingly, the question most often asked by salespeople is, "*when* is the best time to close?". While there is no one answer, there are two distinct situations that signal that it is a good time to close: (1) as soon as you perceive a positive response to your sales presentation, and (2) anytime the customer indicates verbally or non-verbally that he or she has an interest in your product or service.

Sales studies have shown that it takes at least six "no's" in a sales presentation before obtaining that one sweet "yes," therefore, it is imperative that you learn a variety of closing questions:

- Which do you prefer, cash or check?
- In view of the benefits, can you afford to put off this investment until later?
- Would you like to okay this order?
- Don't you agree that anything worth having is worth having now?
- Your pen or mine?
- Would you like it by August 1st or August 15th?
- Would you like me to stop by for the check on Monday?
- How much of a deposit would you like to leave?
- What color do you prefer?
- Will one be enough?
- Would you like it gift wrapped?
- Will we ship it directly?
- Would you prefer early morning delivery?
- Will you be needing accessory items?
- Where would you like it to be installed?

There are dozens of effective closing techniques. Rather than attempt to master a large number of them, learn a few that are consistent with your style. Here are six closing techniques, one of which might be right for you:

1. *Pluses and minuses.* Ask the customer to make a list of pluses and minuses. By the time he or she is finished, it will resemble your original proposal.
2. *Similar situation.* Mention competitors or successful people who have also made a purchase.
3. *Sharp angle close.* If the customer asks, "Will it do this?" respond with the close, "Do you want it if it does?"

4. *Benefits versus price illustration.* On a sheet of paper show the benefits of your product or service in terms of dollar savings over several years. Under that, in a tiny figure, write the selling price of your product or service.

5. *The false exit.* If the customer wants to think it over, make a false exit, then ask, "What better time is there to think it over than right now?"

6. *Assumptive close.* Start filling in the details of the sale during the give and take subsequent to the presentation.

The only way to become a strong closer is to practice. It is better to close too soon and too often rather than too late or infrequently. Closing takes guts, and top salespeople expect to take at least six "no's" while making a presentation.

During a sales presentation, a customer might exhibit a buying signal, indicating that the sale is not far away. Customers who lean forward, ask many questions, or listen intently to your answers are giving you buying signals. As soon as you perceive a positive response, move in to close the sale.

Practically anytime you close is a good time, and the earlier you start closing during a presentation the better off you'll be in the long run. After making a closing statement, stop talking. At this point, silence is golden. Let the customer speak next; you'll have either a sale or an opportunity to continue. Speaking first weakens the impact of the question.

Successful salespeople are strong closers. With each close, you are indicating to the customer that you have confidence, that you see a need for the product and service, and that you and your company are ready to fulfill that need. In that sense, closing is nothing less than assuring the customer that when he reposes his confidence in you and your company, he is making no mistake. And once you prove yourself through carrying out your word in terms of delivery, quality, and other factors, you'll find the next time you meet with this buyer, closing becomes easier. Purchasing agents are people just like the rest of us. The buyers at Apple Computer or General Mills want to be sold. Once you've sold to them, and satisfied them, the ease and likelihood of their making additional purchases from you increases.

Salespeople who can't close are playing a game of luck and hope. They are lucky when they happened to walk into a situation where the prospect is ready to make the purchase. Being lucky or hopeful is certainly worth something. For long-term success, however, closing depends on more than hope, which can be dampened, and luck, which can always turn sour. Only skill stands the test of time.

If you feel that you are a good salesperson in every respect except that you lack the ability to effectively close a sale, don't let another week go by without making plans to learn all you can about closing. Your economic well-being may depend on it. Two well-respected organizations that might be of some help to you are the American Marketing Association, 250 S. Wacker Drive, Chicago, IL 60606 and Sales and Marketing Executives International, Statler Office Tower, Suite 458, Cleveland, OH 44115.

The American Marketing Association is a professional society of marketing and marketing research executives, sales and promotion managers, advertising specialists, teachers, and others interested in marketing. Sales and Marketing Executives International offers sales and marketing management, research, training, and distribution programs.

Learning the buyer's language

To be effective during a sales presentation to corporate purchasing agents, you need to use their language. If you are not communicating in the prospects terms, then you're not communicating at all. Table 4-1 briefly defines some of the terms commonly used in purchasing. But be forewarned, other terminology and methods will replace some of these, and in some companies, entirely different terms are used to describe the same concepts.

Choose your words carefully

Some words, due to the nature of their sound when spoken or the connotations society attaches to them, are better than others for use in a sales presentation. Studies have shown that the following words work well with many customers:

~ own, ownership, possess, invest, investment,
~ save, savings, reserve, occasion, opportunity.

This next set of words often have negative connotations, which tend to detract from the sales presentation:

~ buy, sell, sold, pay, payment, cash, price, deals,
~ pitch, peddle, sign, unload, contract, signature

While it is difficult to avoid using some of these words during a presentation, keep their use to a minimum.

_____Table 4-1._____
Purchasing Parlance

CCM   Centralized Commodity Management. A purchasing program where a commodity manager buys for all plants or divisions regardless of his home base. This eliminates responsibility for commodity purchases by buyers at individual plants and tends to increase contract longevity with the vendor.

CPM   Certified Purchasing Manager. Professional designation awarded by the National Association of Purchasing Management to individuals demonstrating broad experience, competence, and integrity.

JIT   "Just in Time." Refers to a program for reducing cost or eliminating waste by assembling only the minimum resources necessary to add value to a product. Is often mistaken as an inventory program because low inventories is one of the essential elements. Is customer or sales focused rather than production focused.

MRO   Maintenance, Repairs, and Overhaul. Purchasing department expenditures for preservation or enhancement of existing capital assets or resources.

MRP   Materials Requirements Planning. A systematic approach to purchasing that includes forecasting needs, identifying sources, establishing delivery schedules, and monitoring progress.

PM   Purchasing Manager. One who coordinates, directs, and possibly trains buyers and assistant purchasing managers, while also maintaining buying responsibilities.

SIC   Standard Industrial Code. A uniform classification system wherein goods and services are assigned a four digit code. Used by the federal government, particularly the Department of Commerce's Bureau of the Census, as well as private industry.

SPC   Statistical Process Control. A quantitative tool for enhancing quality control relying on probability theory and random sampling to ensure that predetermined standards are maintained.

VA   Value Analysis. An approach to cost reduction in which components are analyzed to determine if they can be redesigned, standardized, or made by less costly methods of production.

Handling objections

La Jolla, California-based Jim Cathcart, CPAE, has provided extensive training in the area of sales techniques and handling objections and has worked with companies such as ITT, General Electric, and Unisys. Cathcart says, "too many salespeople cringe at the thought of objections, often considering them a form of personal rejection. Experienced salespeople, while not encouraging objections, consider them a means of determining what to do to complete the sale."

From a salesperson's perspective, an objection is anything that presents an obstacle to the smooth completion of the sale. They are most concerned about objections in the early part of the sale when they are trying to initiate the relationship, and toward the end, when it comes time to close the sale.

Cathcart observes that too many salespeople react to objections by tensing up. They tend to misinterpret and overreact to them. But salespeople should consider objections not as roadblocks, but rather as "crossroads" to the sale.

Objections are opportunities. By objecting, the prospect is participating in the sale and has told you something. This presents you with an opportunity for increased understanding and more effective tailoring of your sales presentation to the prospect's needs. Objections are like a guidance system. The prospect is saying to you, "Don't go that way. Go this way."

Recognizing objections

"You recognize objections by listening and observing. If you are preoccupied with what you are saying, you'll miss many of the clues the client gives you," says Cathcart. Listen carefully and watch for indications that tell you something is wrong. This could be likened to a stoplight. A person's behavior that says, "no, absolutely not," is like a red light that says, "stop. Do not proceed until you resolve my concern."

Likewise, the person who sends you a "mixed message" is like a yellow light that says, "proceed with caution," because the prospect is evidently not comfortable with what you are saying or doing. The person who gives you positive feedback is like a green light that says, "go ahead, everything is fine."

Effectively handling objections

The following are seven basic techniques that Cathcart has found effective for handling objections.

1. Feel/Felt/Found. "I understand how you FEEL." (I'm empathizing with you.) "Many people have FELT the same way." (You are not alone in feeling this way.) "However, they have FOUND that . . ." Now you present your solution. Here is another way the idea might be used. "I under-

stand your thinking. I thought the same thing when I first saw this product. However, I have found that . . ."

2. Convert to a question. When the prospect makes a statement, many times it is difficult to answer. However, you can convert the statement into a question that allows you to answer it more easily. Example: "I don't think I could use that product." Your response might be, "There is an important question in your statement and that is, 'How can you gain maximum use for a product like this?' Is that the question?" Now you can proceed to answer the QUESTION rather than arguing with the statement.

3. Echo Technique. Sometimes you are faced with a response that doesn't give you enough information. In this case, you can reflect or echo it back to the prospect. The prospect might say that the price is too high. Here you can respond by saying, "Too high?" He or she will generally give you more feedback and information at that point. From there, you can address the concern about price from the prospect's perspective.

4. Lowest common denominator. In this case, you take an objection which has a big image in the prospect's mind and reduce it to a figure much easier to comprehend and handle. Example: "$300 is too much." Response: "$300 does seem like a large price tag until you consider that you will probably be using this 3,000 times a year. This means that your cost per usage is only 10 cents, a small price to pay for the increased convenience and profitability that comes from this product."

5. Boomerang technique. Think of a boomerang and what it does. Once thrown, it makes a wide arc and comes immediately back to the individual who threw it. You do this same thing with a prospect's concern. He or she says, "I'm too busy right now to implement this new procedure." You boomerang it back, "The fact that you are too busy today means that you need the time savings that will come to you as a result of using this product."

6. Change the base. Change the basis upon which the prospect is founding the response so that he or she can see things in a different light. Example: The prospect says, "This won't perform the X-process." Your response: "You were interested in this because it does the Y-process so

well. It would be nice if it did both, but your main concern is the Y-process, isn't it?''

7. Compensation technique. Sometimes an objection is based on a very real shortcoming that must be acknowledged. Example: "This unit is too large for the space." Your reply could be, "I agree that it is larger than the present space, but the benefits are so great that it wouldn't be right to deny them to yourself simply to avoid moving to another space." Admit the shortcoming but override it with added benefits.

As you encounter objections, your knowledge, skills, and intentions will allow you to choose the right path . . . the path to increased sales and increased personal satisfaction.

Selling softly

"Selling softly" sounds like a contradiction in terms. However, David H. Sandler, a sales seminar trainer from Stevenson, Maryland, believes that contrary to most popular conceptions, the supersalesman is a softseller, not a hardseller. He says and does the unexpected and, as a result, gets the customer to reveal important concerns. Then he tailors the pitch to meet those wants and makes the sale. Marks of the super sales professional:

- Brings up objections before the customer thinks of them.
- Doesn't try to impress the customer about how much he knows about his product. Concentrates completely on what will make the sale.
- Spends the first part of the sales meeting asking questions about the customer's problems.
- Spends most of the rest of the time getting the customer to suggest how the problems might be lessened.
- Then makes the sale presentation, tailored to the customer's needs.
- If the customer is hostile, gently tries to neutralize him. If that doesn't work, doesn't try to sell, but lays the foundation for a callback.

The purchasing agent who gives you a hard time on Monday, might have repented by Thursday! I was once kicked out of a company because a sales representative from my firm had previously oversold them and had not adequately installed the equipment.

Dismayed, I made my way slowly out the door, only to be called back, just before getting into my car. The prospect had a change of heart and conceded that my integrity and his present need overruled his initial, emotional response. Those toughest to sell to often become strong advocates later after you've lived up to your words through action. So stand your ground even on the toughest sales calls. Your missionary efforts may ultimately yield a songbird that sings the praises of your products and services to others.

Persistence

You might be a truly talented person, but if you're not making a sufficient number of in-person sales visits, your marketing program will suffer. It is essential to properly work the prospect list that you have developed. Proper use of the list means calling all parties, using spaced intervals between calls. It also means calling everyone on the entire list and not letting the result of the first few calls dampen the enthusiasm you might have generated originally. Wang Laboratories, Figgie International, and Eastern Airlines have sustained large losses over the last few years. It is entirely possible that their purchasing people might not be as receptive as Merck's, Domino's, or Compaq's who have been profitable, but they all have purchasing needs. The point is to hang in there.

It is not unusual for salespeople to place too much reliance on lists that haven't been kept up-to-date or have aged. Any list will be 20 percent outdated within a year.

The average sale is made after the prospect has said "No" six times! If the world's best sales professionals experience six "No's" per prospect before getting a sale, who are we to assume that our selling efforts will require less to be successful?

How supersellers sell

How do supersellers do it? How do they earn $200,000, $400,000, and $600,000 or more per year? Selling, for the balance of the century, chiefly involves *helping* the prospect.

Veteran sales trainer Alan Cimberg believes that selling in the nineties must be synonymous with helping. Buyers want, and are increasingly demanding, significant help, particularly in decision-making from those who sell to them. Supersellers are super helpers. More than ever, salespeople act as consultants to the people to whom they sell and the process of selling has become a two-way street.

Supersellers are constantly on the lookout to help purchasing customers in crucial areas such as cost control, quality improvement, and inventory control. Supersellers help with just in time (JIT) delivery systems, materials requirement planning (MRP), and value analysis (VA). Supersellers point out available product substitutes to prevent massive downtime costs, or help systemize and standardize customer purchases to achieve volume discounts and lower inventory costs.

One Riveria, California, superseller continuously monitors his customer's needs for more functional and cost effective made-to-order packaging. Another superseller arrives on the scene as early as 4:00 a.m. for one customer who checks in at that time. The following items represent a core of traits and behaviors exhibited by many supersellers:

- Offers professional, thorough presentations and timely follow-ups.
- Offers support to buyers within the supplier firm.
- Maintains familiarity with the buyer's product line.
- Maintains expert knowledge of his/her own product line or services.
- Stays abreast of the industry and shares information with buyers.
- Creatively apply their products or services to the buyer's needs.
- Makes regular sales calls.
- Receives a technical education or background.
- Prepares sales calls.

"A winner," according to Denis Waitely, Ph.D. "is someone who never meets you just halfway." Winners go all the way in making sure that the customer or prospect understands how his/her product or service will satisfy the customer's needs. Supersellers look and act like winners.

Managing marketing and sales

Mastering sales techniques ensures an effective performance in the field. Mastery of sales management techniques ensures efficient performance of the overall selling effort, and because sales is the most important component of marketing, of the overall marketing effort. Whether your designated staff or sales representatives master all of the skills previously mentioned, all will be for naught if you cannot effectively manage your company's overall sales effort.

Firms that are successful marketing to corporate giants characteristically document their strength through the use of capability statements, company brochures and sales literature. They have defined their target markets well in advance, collected research or background information on selected targets and, most important, follow a weekly plan. They are able to respond quickly to new opportunities as they become evident while still maintaining a methodical approach to penetrating the market.

My observation in working with more than 250 companies since 1975 is that successful firms are not overly reliant on a few large clients. Instead, they strive to achieve a balanced client mix. Some, though not the majority, employ aggressive promotional techniques to bolster their marketing efforts. Among those smaller vendors who are effective marketers, a designated marketing coordinator is installed to carry out the ongoing program of calling on corporate prospects.

Hiring marketing help

One of the hallmarks in the evolution of an emerging firm is when the entrepreneur recognizes he/she must add a marketing manager or sales staff because the entrepreneur can't do it all alone.

Bill Sharer, Executive Vice President of Exxel Management and Marketing Corporation, Flemington, New Jersey, says that "Done well, hiring salespeople is a risky, imperfect process." "After all," says Sharer, "you are examining someone's past, but hiring his or her future. Done poorly, staff selection is a horror show."

Years of training and experience still do not guarantee uniformly good results. Little wonder that even seasoned entrepreneurs approach the task with trepidation. But, denotes Sharer, careful attention to, and avoidance of, the most common mistakes improves one's odds dramatically.

Sharer noted the following common mistakes entrepreneurs make when seeking sales support, along with their antidotes.

1. Cloning. Many managers tend to hire in their own image and likeness believing that they can best relate to people who share their values, interests, and background. Duplicating yourself might simplify interpersonal relationships, but do nothing to ensure sales effectiveness. People who think differently than you do might be better for your orga-

nization. They might be harder to manage, but the best salespeople often are.

Cloning leads to gamesmanship. People who are like you know your vulnerable points and can exploit them. In its advance stages, cloning becomes a corporate incest and creates a situation where no new ideas emerge because everyone accepts your thinking as the "one true faith."

2. Piracy. If your source of sales talent is from competitors, you play a risky game. Piracy erodes overall market credibility. Salespeople who move from one vendor to the next can arouse customer suspicion and reflect badly on your company's integrity. Piracy also assumes that someone who was successful across the street will be successful with you. That can be a shortsighted assumption. A person who leaves a position for a better offer sometimes continues to search for another that's better still.

3. Chicken or egg hang-up. Should you hire good technicians and teach them to sell or hire good salespeople and teach them the technical aspects of the job? Either strategy can succeed. Your training capability is the key. Which are you better able to teach? Except in highly technical fields, product knowledge is usually easier to teach. So it's often best to select a salesperson.

People who know how to sell and like to sell will learn what they need to know about products, markets, and applications because this knowledge is a means of reaching their goals.

4. Hiring the non-salesperson. Previous sales experience is not an absolute must—everyone has to start somewhere— but a desire to sell is. Beware of anyone who doesn't really want to sell. These people are usually easy to spot: the candidate who is looking at a half-dozen career options; the candidate with no understanding of the selling environment; or an applicant who has vague reasons for choosing sales, such as the desire to work independently, to meet people, to travel, or to earn big money.

Look for evidence of assertiveness, professional aggressiveness, and a clear desire to sell.

5. Stereotypes. To hire good salespeople, you might have to change some deep-seated beliefs. Give every applicant a chance to present his or her case. Listen fairly and objec-

tively. Question what troubles you, but don't just try to justify your emotional perceptions.

Studies show that interviewers usually make a decision in the first five minutes, then spend an hour searching for evidence to support it. That's not only discrimination, it's self-defeating. Supersellers come in all shapes, sizes, and genders!

6. Overselling the opportunity. Interviewers often glamorize the opportunity they offer. This practice is dangerous, especially since salespeople tend to be goal oriented. Many candidates who accept an ''inflated'' offer quickly become disgruntled and leave.

7. The ''best available'' trap. After a lengthy search and many rewarding interviews, managers sometimes choose the ''best available'' candidate, even when they know he/she is unsatisfactory. Most often, you'd be better off with a vacant territory than one filled with an incompetent. There are many strategies preferable to adding a known or probable loser to your staff; temporary assignment, phone coverage by inside staff, direct mail, territory realignment, or major account maintenance by you. Don't hire someone you have serious doubts about, even if he/she is the best of the candidates.

8. Gullibility. People seeking work are often under stress. Job searches can be discouraging and humiliating. It's human nature to present oneself as favorably as possible. And yet, many interviewers accept what applicants say without even trying to verify it. One study showed that Harvard had no record of 4 percent of the job candidates whom employers had sought to verify. Check the references of any candidate to whom you intend to make an offer. Because sales is a high-interface profession, try for a cross-section of references; boss, subordinates, peers, customers, and personal acquaintances.

Consider a character and credit check too, if the position is sensitive or if you uncover anything you consider suspicious. If you doubt the value of reference checks, try secondary sources; contact the reference provided, and then ask who else knew your candidate. The second person, who probably does not expect your call, may be far more candid and, therefore, helpful.

9. Lack of system. If your overall personnel policies are hap-
hazard, your hiring practices are likely to follow suit. Many
companies have vague definitions of success, poor or no
standards of performance, and loose or no appraisal procedures. If you can't say what on-the-job success is, it's
doubtful you'll hire someone who can achieve it.

You should state objective performance expectations for 30,
60, 90 day, and six-month periods. As new employees meet each
bench mark, recognize and reward them. As they don't, weed
them out. There are no shortcuts to good selection. "But the better the job you do," says Sharer, "the less frequently you'll have to
do it, and the easier your day-to-day management will be."

Training your sales staff

Even if you are able to select the best possible person for your sales
staff, you still need to supply some type of training. This is particularly true in the case of somebody hired from outside your company. Progressive purchasing departments in companies such as
Xerox, Raytheon, and Honeywell commit substantial time and
resources developing first-rate purchasing systems and staff. Consequently, you must be no less committed to developing your own
professional sales staff.

At a minimum, you will want to acquaint sales staffers with
your company's history, its organization, and your policies and
procedures. Sales reps must also be thoroughly familiar with your
products and/or services, materials used in their production, design features, and performance capabilities. Once you have
imparted information about your products and/or services you
must also provide what other information you can on products
and services of competitors.

Your training program must also focus on customers. Who
they are, where they are located, and what their needs are. Your
company's history of calling on customers as well as its successes
and failures should be carefully detailed to the sales staff. They will
need to know this in order to effectively represent you.

Depending on your product or service, the size of your staff,
and your target market, your sales staff will be responsible for the
following:

- Providing marketing information and feedback to you.

- Handling customer inquiries and following up on requests.

- Learning the nuances of corporate purchasing processes.
- Negotiating and closing on sales.
- Finding new applications for existing products and services.
- Relaying information to customers.
- Providing training to customers, personnel in effectively using your product or service.
- Representing you at meetings.
- Scouting the competition's goods and services.
- Handling customer complaints.
- Developing and maintaining good customer rapport.
- Seeking and obtaining new accounts.
- Collecting payments.
- Maintaining desired levels of service.
- Finding new ways to satisfy customer needs.
- Maintaining a professional image with prospects and customers.
- Effectively representing your company at all times.
- Maintaining visibility with selected targets.

One veteran corporate purchasing executive observed, "purchasing's responsibility is to get all of the information it can, evaluate it, and make decisions as to whom it wants to do business with." Your primary responsibility in managing the sales function is to hire, train, motivate, and evaluate sales representatives to carry out their assigned selling task effectively. You are responsible for setting salaries and bonuses, establishing sales quotas, and evaluating sales performance.

Establishing sales quotas and territories

Ideally, the sales quotas that you establish for each sales representative and their assigned territories directly follow your marketing plan. Realistically, in the day-to-day operations of your business, this type of coordination is difficult to achieve. Use your revenue forecast as the basis for establishing sales quotas and dividing up territories.

For companies with good track records, the forecast is often based on the trend of previous annual revenues. The major problem with this method is that future sales are predicted largely by what you have done in the past. More often, a revenue target is simply based on the entrepreneur's experience and observation, and forces are then marshalled to achieve that sales figure.

If you forecasted sales of $2,400,000 for the coming 12 months, and your average sales is $50,000, then you will need 48 sales to achieve your sales forecast or roughly four sales per month, although seasonal variations and other factors usually create havoc with such schedules. If a sales representative can effectively make six presentations a week, or 300 a year, and your sales history shows that roughly 5.3 percent of your presentations ultimately turn into sales, then you will need three, full-time salespeople:

$$300 \text{ presentation/yr} \times 5.3\% \text{ closing rate } = 16 \text{ sales}$$

$$48 \text{ sales/yr} - 16 \text{ sales/sales rep } = 3 \text{ sales reps}$$

In this scenario, your average sales rep would bring in roughly $800,000 worth of business:

$$16 \text{ sales} \times \text{ average } \$50,000 \text{ per sale } = \$800,000$$

At a straight eight percent commission, each rep would earn $64,000.

In making territorial assignments, your job would be to divide your target area into three areas so that each territory provided roughly the same potential as the others. This is not an easy task. Also, the way in which you divide your territory might not be by geography but instead by customer characteristics, potential size of order, or any one of a number of other important criteria.

Major computer manufacturers such as Apple, IBM, and Digital Equipment generally assign sales territories by type of customer within regional areas. So, for example, Digital Equipment sales reps in the Washington, D.C. area might cover the defense market while others cover the federal government in general and commercial markets. Territory allocation should be periodically modified to reflect the dynamic nature of the marketplace and the needs of your firm.

Too few companies bother to ask their salespeople for their opinions and then follow up on those suggestions. Giving recognition, it is argued, is a proven method for ensuring that the sales force is, and stays, motivated. "Salespeople," says one veteran sales trainer, "have their ears tuned to the customer, their feet planted in the marketplace, and their minds alert to information about the product, price points, customers, and competitors. No one knows the marketplace or the buyer better."

Evaluating the competition

Many of the marketing research sources and techniques discussed in chapter 6 can be applied in the area of evaluating your competition. Three particularly inexpensive methods that can easily be undertaken include the brochure scan, the phone book scan, and the literature scan.

Brochure scan

An easy and convenient way to learn what your competitors are offering is to send for their brochures, marketing literature, and capability statements. In a free enterprise system, one of the chief sources of competitor information very often is the competitor. It is not unethical to request the brochure of an establishment open for business, and the odds that your brochure, flyers, and other materials have already made it into the hands of your competitors is high.

On the major corporate level, you can bet the farm that electronics rivals such as Litton Industries and North America Philips try to learn as much about each other as possible, as do rubber products producers such as B.F. Goodrich, Goodyear Tire and Rubber, and Uniroyal.

Continuously monitoring your competitors new products and services is a good way to remain competitive. As you read the literature of your rivals, note any specific benefits and features that they offer that you don't. Also, compare the brochures. Which ones appeal to you and why? Are photos helpful and eye-catching? What colors and texture of papers seem to work best?

Phone book scan

Open your phone book to the yellow pages and find your industry. Read all of the information in all of the advertisements placed by your competitors. You might want to classify the items listed by "products and services" and "benefits and features." Use two separate pieces of paper if necessary.

Next, list every product and service offering that any of the companies in your industry advertise. You will end up with a composite list of what your industry has to offer. If available, obtain phone books of other major metropolitan areas. Obviously, no one vendor offers everything on the list you have generated.

Apply the same technique for benefits and features. For example, one feature of working with ABC Company might be that they have been in the same location for 24 years, thus indicating stability. Another benefit of working with the ABC Company might be that they have an 800 number or that they are on call 24 hours a day.

When this list is completed, you will have a composite of all the benefits and features your industry offers as an aggregate. Both the "products and services" list and the "benefits and features" list can help you to decide what mix your company will offer.

The literature scan

The literature scan is the third quick method for scanning the competition. Reviewing the Business Periodicals Index (contained in any library), monitoring regional and local business tabloids, and maintaining a newspaper clipping file will enable you to generate information on your competitors at very little cost.

Keeping up with the marketplace

Seeking new customers is both time-consuming and essential. The continuous turnover of purchasing agents adds to the difficulty and cost of calling on corporate agents. Author and marketing guru, Professor Philip Kotler, points to industrial magazine circulation records at McGraw-Hill. Out of every 1,000 paid subscribers in a 12 month period, 304 are replaced, 56 change titles due to promotions and reorganization, 141 are transferred to different locations, and only 499, approximately half, stay in the same job.

Some 20 years ago, a classic McGraw-Hill advertisement highlighted the problems that sales reps face in trying to maintain information on customers and prospects, and similarly keeping new purchasing agents familiar with the name of your company and your products and/or services. The McGraw-Hill advertisement depicted a sales rep facing a corporate purchasing agent with the purchasing agent's thoughts running as follows:

I don't know who you are.
I don't know your company.
I don't know your company's products.
I don't know what your company stands for.
I don't know your company's customers.
I don't know your company's record.
I don't know your company's reputation.
Now what was it you wanted to sell me?

Kotler points out that what the advertisement was really suggesting was that sales reps should not be forced to use their time and skill to answer questions that could better be handled through mass selling—advertising.

While significant outlays for advertising are not essential to effectively market to large companies, and in most cases represent inordinate costs to smaller businesses, it is essential to produce a brochure and other marketing support literature and to document your company's experience in a capabilities statement, which is covered in the next chapter.

Managing the marketing and sales effort is a never-ending task. There is always more to be done: new improvements to be made in presentations and supporting materials, new marketing leads to explore, and more follow-ups to be made. If, by now, you have concluded that you need additional sales and marketing help, consider yourself ahead in the game.

5

Creating successful marketing presentations

HAVING THE CAPABILITIES TO SUCCESSFULLY SERVE AS A PRODUCT OR service supplier to major corporations is certainly a prerequisite to calling on them. However, you must be able to *document* your company's ability to do the job. The purchasing agent with whom you will deal will be keenly interested in your capabilities regarding the big three: price, quality, and delivery. Agents will require considerable documentation relating to your firm's history, track record, and capabilities.

This chapter first summarizes the minimum information requirements for a successful marketing presentation—the information you must have in your briefcase and be able to supply upon request—and discusses brochures and other supporting literature. The information on documentation is arranged in 13 topic areas:

- Ownership
- Market served
- Products/services
- Projects/activities

- Management expertise
- Research capabilities
- Labor relations
- Plant and equipment
- Quality assurance
- Financial capabilities
- Price
- Security
- Other documentation

Ownership

A description of ownership is generally the first item in your capability statement. How is your business organized? The purchasing agent or buyer will want to know whether your firm is a sole proprietorship, partnership, or corporation, and indeed supplier application forms that many companies require, such as Grumman or Dow Chemical, ask for form of ownership immediately. In a nutshell, ownership can be classified as:

- sole proprietorships, which are owned by a single individual;
- partnerships, owned by two or more individuals; and
- corporations, legal entities formed under state law.

If your business is a corporation, list the members of your board of directors and the stockholders, including their respective ownership percentages.

If you are a sole proprietorship or a partnership, list the members of your advisory board. Incidentally, if you don't have an advisory board, consider creating one using experienced business people, retired bankers, and/or college professors with specialties in your field, and seek their advice. Have the temerity to solicit those individuals that can make a difference in your business.

If you are a minority business—say so—and elaborate on the percentage of minority ownership. Be sure to mention if your business is certified as a minority-owned firm by federal, state, or local agencies, or by any other organization (e.g., a public utility). Many corporations such as Zenith, Todd Shipyards, General Motors, Northrop, McDonnell Douglas, and Upjohn are receptive to minority-owned business.

Market served

Specify what market you are attempting to serve and why your products/services meet the needs of this market. Many entrepreneurs fluctuate daily making half-hearted attempts to penetrate first one market, then a second, and then a third. They never stop to decide which market they should penetrate first. The quixotic approach simply doesn't work.

An important step in effective prospecting is to set aside time to learn about the operating characteristics of the industry and businesses to whom you wish to sell to. What in your past experience can be drawn upon and used as a competitive advantage in penetrating your chosen market? What do you presently offer that is consistent with the changing needs of the market?

A product or service that fulfills the needs of a specifically defined group is preferable to one that compromises to suit widely divergent needs. By targeting a particular segment, you can tailor your product to more closely serve your customer's needs. The closer the match, the greater the potential for sales. Descriptive terminology in this section might encompass geographic area—climate, terrain, natural resources, population density, cultural values; the usage rate for the product—heavy, moderate, or light; the type of organization; customer size; and use of the product.

For example, one company's market for sales of uniforms consists of corporations, hospitals, laboratories, police departments, fire departments, fast food chains, grocery store chains, municipal workers (e.g., sanitation workers, road crews), and prisons in a 200 mile radius of its mill.

Products/services

At the Boeing Corporation, the hard copy documentation for a 747 aircraft outweighs the plane! Whatever you are offering can be described a bit more easily. Your firm's products or services should be clearly and completely described, and all of your firm's locations, including addresses and phone numbers, should be listed, including the one at which you can be most readily found.

Are you innovative in your approach to product/service offerings? Innovative means providing better and more economical goods and services than your competitors. The word is that vendors must be involved in almost a partnership type of relationship, in many cases, starting from the design level. If you can, identify features of your product or service that distinguish it and make your firm stand out from the others. Examples of innovation include:

- lower prices
- new and better product—even at a higher price
- new uses for existing products or services
- new design
- new distribution method
- new production method
- new or improved servicing
- new marketing techniques

Innovations specifically for product offerings might also include:

- greater durability
- portability
- ease of replacement
- add-on features
- guarantees beyond industry norms
- extended product life
- consultations
- training
- after hours service

Innovation is as important for service companies as for manufacturing or engineering firms. Innovation in service offerings might include:

- safety guarantees
- accelerated levering
- on-site services
- reduced turn-around time
- dual functions
- special requests

Projects/activities

A concise description of recent projects on which your firm has performed well should be included in this section (see Fig. 5-1). If you have references or testimonial letters commending your firm

CLIENT: Pacific Coast Aerospace Corporation

PROJECT DESCRIPTION:

Phase 1   Feasibility study and recommendations which included:

—Survey of existing systems
—Current and future application requirements
—Analysis of requirements
—Systems cost/analysis of competing hardware
—Operational and communications requirements
—Development of functional specifications
—Development of procurement package.

Phase 2   Selection, procurement, and installation of equipment included:

—Equipment Selection, Procurement Management
—Installation and Component Testing
—Communications and Interfaces
—Development of all Operational
—Guides/Procedures
—Orientation and Training
—Data Conversion, Maintenance
—Establishment of a Prototype Automated Office Center.

CLIENT: MidWest Manufacturer and Distributor

ABC Systems developed a software package for a DEC system to inventory office and other spaces by type, create a file of company personnel by title and office, and collect data identifying the degree of interaction between offices. ABC also developed a model for the optimum location and allocation of space; the optimum being defined as the location and allocation that would result in weighted, minimum slack time related to interaction among offices. This effort involved:

—Data analysis
—Creation of large data files and routines for file manipulation
—Mathematical analysis using the theory of graphs
—Software development
—System documentation

Fig. 5-1. Project descriptions of work performed by a systems installation firm.

your firm and the job you have done, be sure to include these. Purchasing agents like to know up front who else you've done business with. Obtain permission from satisfied customers to use their names for references for potential new customers. Describe your firm, including how long your firm has been in business.

Management expertise

The management expertise section should include resumes of the key members of your organization, outlining their training, education, and experience. How long has each member been with your firm? Your public library has books to guide you in preparing resumes and illustrating various formats. A uniform style for the resumes will enhance the professional image of your firm.

Research capabilities

If your company does research, explain specifically what your capabilities include. This is important and could enhance your chances as a prospective supplier.

Labor relations

Describe the composition of your labor force. What is the average length of employment? If you have valued, long-term employees, it demonstrates the stability of your work force, good working conditions, and most important, the probability of the continued availability of these people to your company.

Are your employees unionized? If your employees are unionized, a potential buyer might associate their higher skill levels with higher labor costs. To a potential buyer, the threat of a strike could prevent delivery of his orders. If there have not been any strikes at your company be sure to include this point.

Is your business located in a state with right-to-work laws? Right-to-work laws prohibit "union shops," which require new employees to join the union. Wages might be lower with potentially lower labor costs. Are your employees paid minimum wage? This might indicate easily replaceable employees and lower labor costs to a buyer.

Are both skilled and unskilled labor available for your business? A potential buyer wants to know how easily you can enlarge your staff to handle an order. A large labor supply indicates that your current employees will remain with you due to greater competition for available jobs. Manufacturers will particularly need to describe the availability of workers in their area. Also, list the hourly rates of your current employees and the rates of any new additions to your work force that might be necessary on the new contract you are seeking.

Plant and equipment

If appropriate for your firm, list the type of machinery that you use, including capacity, age, and number of each type. Photos of plant or equipment are always helpful.

Also, accurately list the size of your plant or office in square feet and your daily output when operating at your maximum level. This information might be requested by purchasing agents.

Quality assurance

If the customer has specifications you must meet, and nearly all will, explain how you will be checking your product or service to determine whether it adheres to specifications. One way to demonstrate the integrity of your product/service is to offer a guarantee or warranty. If you do guarantee your service, describe the scope and how you will uphold it. Federal Express became famous for guaranteeing delivery of your package "when it absolutely, positively has to be there overnight." Now that is some guarantee and a magnificent obsession with commitment.

The wording of any guarantees or warranty should be checked with an attorney to ensure that you are not getting in over your head. Guarantees and warranties are strong marketing tools that can enhance your selling effort.

Big corporations want to know about your quality control program, (see chapter 10). At Scott Paper Company, close relationships with a few quality, control-conscious vendors has paid off in both improved quality and lower cost. If your firm has an established program to monitor the quality of production, or level of service provided, briefly describe it and the benefits to the recipient. Itemize any equipment used for testing and inspection and explain the tolerance, range, or capacity of the equipment employed.

Financial capability

Though you would probably prefer not to supply financial capability information, the corporate representative with whom you deal with will request a copy of your latest balance sheet, profit and loss statement, and line of credit information, if applicable. Others might also require your financial statements for the past three years. Even if your statements do not appear as healthy as you would like them to be, you cannot avoid this requirement. Thus, it pays to have them readily available. (See chapter 11 for help in strengthening your financial position.)

Price

The price of your product or service depends on many variables. A successful marketing presentation will identify and itemize factors affecting price, including:

- Initial charge
- Development charges
- Engineering charges
- Tooling charges
- Special equipment charges
- Testing charges
- Material charges
- Machine rates

A one-paragraph description of why the customer will be obtaining a good value for the price you are charging will bolster your presentation. To meet the challenge of competition, offer your best price, along with your best quality and your best delivery date. While remaining competitive, you must strive to attain a minimum of deviation from the customer's requirements and your plans to meet them.

Security

You must be prepared to explain how you will guarantee that trade secrets, confidential information, or new product and service plans will not be divulged. Also, describe in detail the security measures in place for your plant, office, storage yard, or other facilities. How does your firm safeguard important documents, and who has responsibility for maintaining security? Your firm's ability to provide a high level of security to private-sector corporations will enhance your marketing position. This is particularly true if you deal with federal defense or aerospace contractors such as Rockwell International or United Technologies.

Other documentation

Make sure your firm's organizational chart and the proposed organization for the specific project are available. How does your firm handle regulation and legal compliance? Cite any regulations—federal, state or, local—that you are required to meet and how you plan to meet them. This information helps convey that you are "on top of the situation."

Comprehensively and accurately documenting your company's capabilities will assume greater importance as more corporate purchasing divisions are able to catalog suppliers electronically. Forecasters predict that today's electronic data information (EDI) systems within corporate divisions will soon give way to bigger enterprise systems capable of handling all types of supplier-related information. As EDI systems gain popularity within corporate purchasing departments, supplier capabilities and historical performance becomes a matter of permanent and readily accessible record.

Some corporations use EDI systems to maintain a formal buyer certification process that can monitor such key areas as cost, delivery, and quality. Other companies add key components such as reliability, potential savings, and manufacturing expertise. These systems enable purchasing staffs to gain quick access to data to improve overall performance. Parker Hannifin Corporation, for example, with over $2.5 billion in sales in 1989 has established a management information system that evaluates and compares more than 75,000 suppliers from the United States and Canada.

A purchasing agent using a desktop terminal at Parker can call up on his screen all of the commodities a particular supplier offers, or get a comparison of all suppliers that sell a particular commodity. Other screens might provide information on delivery, quality, goods, and prices. The Parker system can also quickly identify local suppliers in areas where the corporation has manufacturing plants.

To make sure all buyers in the company are fully adept at using this information system, Parker developed a week-long course for its purchasing professionals. They also established a newsletter with a brief write-up from each division that includes specific information on suppliers including pricing, delivery, and reliability. This way, supplier performance—both good and bad—within one operating unit of the corporation can be shared by all operating units. The net result for you is, if you are good, more buyers within the company might be giving you a call, and if you are not so good, everyone will know it quickly.

At Pacific Bell, 5,000 vendors supply 16,514 items. Only about 100 of the 5,000 vendors are currently accessible through the Pacific Bell's EDI system although this number will increase each year. These 100 suppliers account for more than 50 percent of the company's total procurement budget.

In all, more than 850 employees at Pacific Bell can use the EDI system, even though not all are within the purchasing department. Many are engineers or field technicians that might need to order small ticket items such as wire, wrenches, or perhaps power tools. These field staff members use passwords and log in numbers to order necessary items. They usually don't have information on names of suppliers, brand, or price—the purchasing department takes care of that.

You cannot avoid the reality that effective marketing to private-sector corporations requires a great deal of documentation. If your reaction to this is, "that's all fine, but we don't have the time to round up all this data," you are effectively cutting yourself from the team. Consider that it is costly and time-consuming for major corporations to prequalify small suppliers, usually *not* because of poor quality in the products or services provided. More often, the problem lies in inadequate documentation, control, and accounting.

Successful suppliers can demonstrate competence in providing quality products and services, and solid capability in the area of management *documentation* and controls. Lack of documentation is a basis by which purchasing agents can easily weed out those firms who might appear incapable of meeting requirements.

Preparing a brochure

In addition to formal documentation, many other printed tools can aid your quest to become a key supplier to corporate giants.

The preparation of an effective brochure is a deceptively difficult task. Your brochure serves as a central source of printed information to existing and potential customers. An effective brochure, at the least, contains basic information on your company's history, philosophy, organizational structure, and service areas. Your brochure should help enhance your image, it literally represents you on paper. It should also be designed to project uniqueness.

Producing your firm's brochure is a complex undertaking and requires significant effort. You lay the groundwork for the development of the brochure, but rely on outside assistance for its completion. The first questions you might ask yourself in undertaking this project are, "What targets do I want to reach?," and "What message do I want to offer?"

A brochure is like an expensive, illustrated calling card. Many vendors end up producing a brochure that perhaps supplies ego gratification, but does not satisfy the information needs of the customer. Your brochure is not for you, it is for your prospects and customers and, thus, should focus on their needs.

In addition to the basic information cited above, a prospective customer will also be interested in learning about:

- The qualifications of your skilled labor force
- The quality of your product or service
- The size and location of your plant or offices
- The range of your services
- Your company's reputation
- Your company's experience in specific industries
- Others who have used your products or services
- How long you've been in business

A quick way to determine what type of brochure will be right for you is to assemble the brochures of all your competitors (if you've undertaken a brochure scan, this will be easy to do) and study their efforts. Writing to companies outside of your trade area might yield better results than writing to those that are potential competitors.

After you've assembled these brochures, carefully review features that appeal to you. There are literally hundreds of factors to consider. The following represent a mere subset of all of the options available in developing your brochure: dimensions, quality of paper, weight (affects mail cost), use of pictures, staff biographies, client lists, number of pages, use of color, use of flaps, pockets, fold overs, use of testimonials, use of bulleted sections, action photos, sketches, style of print, layout, spacing, headings, and titles.

You will eventually need to turn over the development of your brochure to a marketing or graphics specialist. The key to effective use of an outside resource is to supply a rough prototype of your desired end product. Sketch the layout and content of each brochure page to the best of your ability.

In your selection of outside assistance, try to seek marketing or advertising professionals who have experience working with firms similar to yours. Ask to see samples of their work.

Hugo-Dunhill, a division of Mailing List, Inc., reports that brochures that get action are built around benefits prospects will enjoy when they buy your products/services, and are carefully targeted to the right people. Here are eight tips they suggest on brochure preparation:

1. Focus on the prospect's needs and desires—not on your company. It is not your brochure that sells your product/services, it's the benefits your brochure gets across to your prospects that sell.

2. Avoid cliches, fuzzy words, "buzz-words," empty adjectives, and outlandish claims. Busy people respond to straight talk.

3. Use short sentences, active verbs, present tenses, and a lot of "How to's." Draw the prospect into it by making it personal, positive, upbeat, and exciting.

4. Use a compelling layout including lots of white space, strong and closely-related graphics, and many powerful headings. Guide the reader from the front page to the last word: think of it as a road map. Break up the copy into easily read bits.

5. Make it believable by proving every strong claim with data, endorsements, and proof statements from your previous customers.

6. Tell prospects precisely what they will receive and when, where, and how they will receive it. Emphasize "You will get . . .," rather than "We will give you . . ."

7. Make it easy for prospects to tell, at a glance, how they will benefit from what you can do for them.

8. Protect your investment by printing and mailing fewer brochures rather than cutting corners on professionally-produced copy and art work, layout and design, and photography. Use good paper and a top-notch printer. The results are worth the cost.

Harry A. Olson, Ph.D. author of *The New Way to Compete*, believes that any printed material disseminated by your company, "must be a class act." The best brochures, according to Olson "concentrate on what is being offered to the customer," or in other words, the payoff for the target audience. As a small business entrepreneur successfully marketing his services to dozens of major corporations, Olson initially produced what he terms, a completely disastrous brochure. His second, streamlined, more customer-focused brochure won a national design award.

Preparing other supporting literature

Other effective marketing literature that can be used in the marketplace include fact sheets, pamphlets and announcements.

Fact sheets   Fact sheets can consist of nothing more than one page of professionally printed sheets, outlining distinct aspects of your company's operations—a description of the types of problems your customers encounter and how you overcome them; your company's background and corporate history and how your reputation for quality benefits all customers; or specific, detailed information about a product or service that you offer.

Pamphlets   Pamphlets can be produced on a wide variety of topics such as your company's history, the expertise of your staff, a specific product or service offering, or how others have benefited by using your product or services.

Announcements   Announcements may be in the form of bulletins or news or press releases. This type of message is usually singular in focus offering details on an event that will take place, news about your company, news about a specific product or service, or other information. The announcement should be made with an air of urgency. A detailed discussion of marketing support literature is presented in my book, co-authored with Richard A. Connor, Jr., *Marketing Your Consulting and Professional Services*, John Wiley and Sons.

All supporting marketing literature must be developed far in advance of actual sales calls and should be professionally prepared and designed so as to augment and increase the effectiveness of yourself or your sales representatives. Marketing is a numbers game and you will have to make many contacts with corporations to be successful with a few. Therefore, your marketing support literature must be well prepared and produced in sufficient quantities so that it can be distributed to those targeted to be called upon.

6

Targeting corporate giants

As ROBERT CARRINGTON READ HIS MORNING PAPER, HE NOTICED AN item of particular interest. A multinational firm headquartered in the next county had announced an expansion of their product line to include hydraulic brakes. Rob owns and manages a firm that produces the components that could be used in these brake assemblies.

Navigating the corporate maze

Recognizing a potentially large new market for his components, Rob called corporate headquarters to speak with the purchasing people. The receptionist informed him that no purchasing personel are located at the headquarters of the firm. Rob then asked for the correct location to call and was placed on hold while the receptionist checked. Because this was a long distance call, Rob counted the dollars as the minutes passed. The receptionist finally returned with the name of the east coast plant where purchasing activities took place and gave Rob the phone number—another long distance call.

Rob was tenacious. Knowing that this was a solid marketing lead for his firm, he called the east coast plant. More time and money was spent as Rob and the receptionist attempted to identify the correct purchasing manager for this new product line.

Success at last! Rob was connected with the proper office only to be told that this purchasing manager circulates through the region and would be in Tennessee for three weeks. Rob got the telephone number for the Tennessee plant and placed his third long distance call. He located the purchasing manager and began his "sales pitch" for the components he produced. Unfortunately, this purchasing manager was not the right person after all. He told Rob that he would have to talk with someone else.

Navagational tools

This probably sounds painfully familiar to you. You run through the corporate maze spending time and money and get nowhere. It is tough to navigate through corporate channels. A purchasing manager for Exxon, one of the nation's major oil refineries, admitted that he has trouble finding the right people within his own corporation.

There are steps you can take to make this process easier. "Fishing" attempts by telephone, such as Rob's, almost always lead to frustration. Rob had the right idea to follow up a marketing lead but chose the wrong way to do it. If you have the corporate headquarter's address, here are three simple ways to navigate the corporate maze:

1. *Seek supplier guides.* Write to the purchasing department to receive copies of any supplier guides (chapter 10), supplier application forms, and a list of products purchased. If the purchasing department address is not available, send the letter in care of corporate headquarters.

2. *Ask for corporate news.* Write to the public relations office for copies of the company's newsletter, in-house publications (Fig. 6-1), and any recent press releases on what the company is doing. These services might contain useful information that can help you tailor your marketing pitch. You can request one sample copy of any in-house publication. It's not likely that you'll be put on the mailing list. However, the sample(s) you receive will certainly give you a sense of how the company operates and some of the things it values.

Moonbeams

Contents

Lowering the Boom on Product Damage

What Have You Got to Lose?

CORPORATE BUILDINGS
EDITOR
Lisa Hulse

SALES EDITOR
Greg Sanders

PLANTS EDITOR
Bob Schoellkopf

ART DIRECTOR
John Reece

Corporate Buildings Moonbeams
Sales Moonbeams
SY-6 P.O. Box 599
Cincinnati, Ohio 45201

Plants Moonbeams
Ivorydale Technical Center
5299 Spring Grove Avenue
Cincinnati, Ohio 45217

© 1990
The Procter & Gamble Company
Printed in the U.S.A.

Fig. 6-1. A contents page for a Procter & Gamble in-house publication. © The Procter & Gamble Company. Used with permission.

3. *Small Business Liaison Office.* Write a letter to the small business coordinator explaining your product or service and your interest in becoming a supplier to the corporation. Raytheon, Dow Corning, Owens-Illinois, and 3M, among hundreds of others, provide names and phone numbers of plants and purchasing agents. Not all firms have a coordinator, nevertheless, you will receive a response indicating the name, title, and location of a person who can handle your request.

Only a few handwritten letters are needed to obtain materials that contain a wealth of information. Determine the appropriate division, plant, and persons to call. The more you can narrow your search, the better. And the more you know about the company you're calling on and the trends in the industry, the better.

Becoming your own quick study

The following are additional data you can obtain to gain vital data information about corporate targets:

Annual reports and 10k reports   To obtain annual reports and 10k reports, you must first obtain the address of corporate headquarters. This can be done by telephone if you know the city in which the company is located. You could also look up the corporate address in *Moody's, Dun & Bradstreet,* or *Standard & Poor's Index,* all located in the business reference section of libraries. Better yet, simply call the reference desk of your local library. They'll give you the address over the phone. Then write to the company's shareholder information office and ask for a copy of the annual report. The annual report might contain addresses and phone numbers of various plant sites or divisions. Annual reports usually have three distinct areas that can yield valuable marketing research information:

1. Chief executive officer's report:
    ~ Expansion plans
    ~ Warning of "streamlining" operations (possible indication of closing some facilities)
    ~ New social responsibility or awareness programs
    ~ New product lines
    ~ Diversification
2. Consolidated income statements:
    ~ Track net revenue over time
    ~ Track percentage change over time
    ~ Observed increases or decreases
3. Auditor's letter:
    ~ Exceptions or notes to financial statements
    ~ Any "one-time" accounting entries
    ~ Changes in accounting methods

A walk through Corning's 1989 annual report, for example, reveals that the company is coming off of a five-year record period for net income, they have decided to abandon several cyclical or mature businesses such as light bulb glass, refractory blocks, passive electronic components, and specialized ceramics. They formed a partnership with ASAHI Glass of Japan.

Four acquisitions during the 1980s—MetPath, Hazelton, U.S. Precision Lens, and Revel Ware are all thriving. Looking ahead, Corning sees the most dynamic world markets by the year 2000 to be medicine, health, leisure, information technology, and opto-electronics. The company is proceeding full speed ahead in the areas of optical fiber, consumer housewares, Steuben crystal, cellular ceramics, flood lamps, and architectural lighting.

Corning employees have absorbed 1.5 million hours of training in five years to make the company's "Total quality" system pay great dividends. In all, the 20-page annual report is a bonanza for the supplier who is calling on a corporate purchasing agent from Corning for the first time.

A walk through the 1989 Quaker Oats annual report reveals similar types of information, arranged by:

- letters from top officers to shareholders;
- comprehensive financial information and operations review (by product, division, and financial performance); and
- standard corporate information such as corporate headquarters, transferring agent, auditors, exchanges where shares are listed, shareholder services, investor relations, media relations, and the consumer affairs department.

In addition to corporate annual reports, you can also obtain a 10k report. The Securities and Exchange Commission requires that this publicly owned corporate giant file an annual 10k report. This document expands on information contained in the annual report and includes additional documentation and "hard numbers." These might be requested from the commission for a fee, or from the corporation at no cost, although corporations do not send out 10ks as willingly as they do annual reports.

Purchasing one share of stock is a relatively inexpensive and effective method of obtaining annual reports, 10k's, quarterly reports, and entrance to shareholders' meetings.

Associations Associations are an excellent resource too. A professional or trade association exists for every industry and type of business. Appendix C contains a sampling of associations. Most associations maintain a membership directory, which can provide a ready-made target list for you. Although, some associations do not release their membership directory to nonmembers.

Some associations administer a professional referral system, whereby key individuals with specific expertise within the industry can be identified. Using an association referral system for industries that require high technology or highly specialized suppliers is an excellent way to become less "hard to find."

Association directories can be found in any library and offer the names, addresses, and phone numbers of your industry's trade and professional associations. Two association directories collectively offer over 10,000 listings: Gales Encyclopedia of Associations and the National Trade and Professional Associations (NTPA).

Newspaper indexes If you want to find an article or information on a corporation that appeared in your local newspaper, your public library will often have a newspaper index that abstracts newspaper articles by topic and cross-references this listing by date. Your metro area might also be served by one or more area business publications. You can write to the Association of Area Business Publications, 202 Legion Drive, Annapolis, MD 21401, for the complete list.

The *Wall Street Journal Index* is available in many public libraries in major cities. If you want to identify a specific industry or trade journal, consult *Gebbie's All-in-One Directory, Bacon's Publicity Checker,* or the *Standard Periodicals Directory.*

Scores of other publications are available that can further aid you in your research on target corporations. Standard and Poor's *Register of Directors and Executives* offers the names, businesses, and home addresses of 75,000 top executives with biographies-in-brief that list their directorships showing interlocking business affiliations and alma maters.

The *Register's* corporate listings give you the type of businesses, zip-coded addresses, telephone numbers, and, in most cases, the approximate annual sales and number of employees. A substantial number of listings also identify company accountants, primary banks, and primary law firms.

The *Thomas's Register of American Manufacturers*, Thomas Publishing Company, is a multivolume reference source that lists manufacturers' sources alphabetically by state and the city within the state. Trade and brand names are also given alphabetically, along with company names, addresses, and a variety of other information. This book is good for locating the source of brand names and providing sources for your goods, as well as giving you details on companies you might want to contact.

Dun and Bradstreet's *Middle Market Directory* lists more than 31,000 companies with net worths ranging from $500,000 to $999,999, presented alphabetically by name and geographically by business address. It includes the company size, chief executives, products, and financial information.

The Corporate 1000, published by Monitor, provides facts on the top 1,000 manufacturing and service corporations in the United States and enables readers to easily locate every key executive and every prime purchasing and decision-making individual. Also, suppliers' guides, often called blue books or red books, can be found in the business reference section of many public libraries. For example, the *Blue Book of Metro Area Home Builders* and the *Red Book of Plumbing Supply Contractors* are often issued by the local associations serving these industries.

Information from Uncle Sam   The federal government is one of the largest publishers in the world. Through the Bureau of Census of the Department of Commerce, you can obtain sales and revenue data on virtually any industry, by state, county, and standard metropolitan statistical area. Although the Census Bureau is primarily known for its population reports, a business census is taken on the second and seventh year of each decade and is generally available 18 months thereafter.

Census information is provided on more than 800 of the approximately 1,000 industries, businesses, and products according to the Standard Industrial Code system. Expense and production type information was collected for about 1,000 material categories and quantity and value data for 16,000 product classifications. Separate censuses were conducted for manufacturers, mineral industries, construction industries, retail trade, wholesale trade, and service industries. For more information, write to Superintendent of Documents, U.S. Government Printing Office (GPO), Washington, D.C. 20402.

The Department of Commerce annually publishes the *U.S. Industrial Outlook,* which traces the growth of 200 industries and provides five-year forecasts for each industry. The *U.S. Statistical Abstract* is a compilation of data and reports from the Department of Labor, the Department of Transportation, the Small Business Administration, and other federal agencies.

State information sources   Nearly every state has their own Department of Commerce, and nearly all have special offices established to assist small or disadvantaged businesses. The state capital, state capital library, and the governor's office, as well as the offices of your elected officials, often maintain special reports, studies, and analysis that might prove useful in your marketing research efforts.

Newsletters   Newsletters have become a valuable source of marketing research information. Newsletters are now published by virtually every corporation. The *Oxbridge Newsletter Directory* lists several thousand newsletters, arranged by functional area. The *National Trade and Professional Association Directory* (NTPA) indicates which of the thousands of associations listed maintain a newsletter. The *Newsletter Yearbook* is also a valuable guide. By accessing these directories and others, your local librarian may suggest, you can gain access to late-breaking news and information of concern to your business and your industry.

If you have a computer and modem, you can subscribe to hundreds of business-oriented newsletters, even if you are not a subscriber to any of them through NewsNet. NewsNet is an information delivery and retrieval service that produces electronic editions. Current newsletter issues and back issues for the past year are stored in NewsNet's main computer. By dialing a local telephone number, NewsNet users access that data base. They pay a modest rate to read the newsletters.

There are two other features available without additional charge. Subscribers are able to scan headlines only, allowing them to be selective with the articles, thus reducing time charges. Additionally, any newsletter, a combination of newsletters, a date, a combination of dates, or the entire data base can be searched by keyword. You select a word or words and order the computer to search for articles containing that word or both words. It then tells you which articles contain the word or words selected, allowing you to scan headlines or read the selected articles. More information is available from NewsNet, 945 Haverford Road, Bryn Mawr, PA 19010, (800) 345-1301.

Local resources Local resources like planning communities, the research department of newspapers, highway commissions, local libraries, and the county courthouse are just a few of the information sources you might want to tap, depending on your research need. Many entrepreneurs have found that a wealth of information can be gained right over the phone or by simply visiting nearby organizations or agencies.

The local chamber of commerce has figures for the types of businesses in your area and estimation of profits, number of new people moving into the area, listings of local media, etc. Both on the local and national level, it is a valuable source of information. Local colleges and universities can also be a useful source of information on the size and accessibility of your market. These institutions can sometimes offer assistance or advice through graduate research programs.

Using data bases

Computerized data bases allow you to gather hard-to-find information on small industrial niche markets. The information is usually difficult to gather using conventional market research tools. Research regarding industrial markets usually involves the need for information on market size, the major players in the market, market growth rate, technological trends, distribution channels, and product pricing.

Data bases generally consist of 500,000 to several million records. Each record is an abstract of a published article, containing several paragraphs that give the major points of the article, along with bibliographic information. Data bases can be searched by specific product names, company names, index terms, or by free-text searching, using pertinent key words in appropriate combinations, such as "residential and commercial and fasteners and molding." Well established data bases such as Dialog, Nexis, Dow Jones News, and virtually every other data base can be located by using:

COMPUTER-READABLE DATABASES
Gale Research Inc.
Book Tower
Detroit, MI 48226

Even the most difficult market can be researched using computerized data bases. If research were being conducted on lunar landing gear, the researcher would use search terminology such as protective garments, industrial garments, or SIC 3842. Data bases also can be used for pricing strategy, distribution channel selection, advertising and promotional budgeting, and requests for venture capital.

Gathering information on the following six essential elements will provide a brief but effective corporate profile. This type of profile affords quick review, updating, and use of sales calls.

1. Operations—an overview of what the company does, including major markets, number of plants, total personnel, and other pertinent information.

2. Sales—sales of the corporation as reflected in its most recent annual report and its ranking within its industry based on lists in *Forbes* or *Fortune*.

3. Outlook—where the corporation is heading, new product and service areas, significant management initiatives, and

other information that indicates the direction of the corporation.

4. Product and services—an in-depth list of the company's products and/or services.

5. Tips for suppliers—information on vendor and small vendor utilization programs, purchasing structure and procedures, specialized buying needs, which you might be able to fulfill, and strategy hints for contacting and marketing the corporation.

6. Contact—name and phone number of the person(s) with responsibility for facilitating supplier marketing efforts within the corporation. If applicable, includes names and phone numbers of divisional purchasing contacts.

Your ability to effectively gather information to support your market planning is directly related to how organized you are. Once you or your staff have become familiar with the reference sources you need, then generating timely, effective marketing research information will become less difficult. Also, you'll get a feel for which giants attempt to assist small suppliers and which could care less.

Identifying friendly giants

Most major corporations have good intentions when it comes to awarding contracts to new suppliers. Unfortunately, not all purchasing managers realize that the corporate procurement cycle—the time from the initial marketing contact to the actual contract award—might take so long that it effectively eliminates many smaller firms from competing for new contracts.

One corporate purchasing executive admitted that the average procurement cycle at his company is 24 months. He said that most large corporations are burdened by contracting procedures that make the procurement cycle a hardship for many smaller suppliers. The following are ways procurement procedures have been modified to be more responsive to smaller business suppliers:

*   Corporations such as Control Data, Pfizer, and McDonnell Douglas predetermine which contracts will be limited to small and small minority businesses. This way, there is ample time to outline qualifications and specifications for the small suppliers.

- Some contracts are earmarked to be sole-source, non-bid proposals and competitive bids for small business vendors. Job size has a lot to do with this determination, along with the availability of capable suppliers with whom the purchasing department is already acquainted. Some corporations develop a list of qualified suppliers from their list of eligible suppliers for each contract—well before contract announcement or proposal solicitation, so that less time is wasted qualifying eligible suppliers.

- The largest portion of time in the procurement cycle is spent determining whether or not a group of small suppliers actually qualifies to perform a particular job. Some firms cut down the number of unqualified proposals submitted by providing small suppliers with a checklist of what they need and don't need to qualify for specific contracts. Also, procurement processing time has been cut in recent years by streamlining forms and other documentation required from small business suppliers.

- Some corporations set priorities for small business procurement, establish time frames favorable to small vendors for job announcements, and bid or proposal deadlines.

- Many corporations are striving for better communication with small vendors. Better communication means less time is required to convey contract needs and there are fewer misunderstandings that lead to delays in the procurement process. Progressive corporations have installed a procurement spokeperson to deal exclusively with small vendors, usually the small business coordinator. With a single representative communicating with the suppliers, inappropriate, unneeded, and time-consuming communications between the wrong parties is often eliminated.

- Corporations are increasingly providing all contract information and specifications in one package to avoid costly revisions and delays for the suppliers.

- Some corporations maintain candor with small suppliers, advising them as soon as possible when their proposals or bids fail to meet qualification standards. This frees up everybody's time. This policy also gives you a chance to move on and concentrate on another opportunity. Also, when you've been informed of why you didn't receive a contract award in timely fashion, you'll tend to think more highly of a responding corporation.

Suppliers guides

An important feature that makes large companies attractive to small suppliers is a well-written, readily available suppliers guide (Figs. 6-2 and 6-3). Moreover, an effective and concise suppliers guide is crucial for any product or service vendor aiming to sell to the giants. Two companies, Unisys and Raytheon, are particularly helpful in this area.

Many corporations take great pride in their supplier/vendor guide, also known as welcome booklets for suppliers. To encourage competition among their readers, *Purchasing Magazine* initiated a "welcome booklet" contest to its readers. The goal was to find the best materials available for helping suppliers understand their corporate customers. Increasingly, corporations are recogniz-

A TYPICAL MESSAGE TO SUPPLIERS

President's Message

This booklet will serve as a guide for prospective suppliers to us. In it they will find the policies and procedures we believe best enable us to work effectively with them.

Suppliers are a very important part of our organization. Our ability to satisfy customer needs depends on the quality of the products and services that our vendors supply and on the timeliness of their delivery. For that reason, our goal is to establish relationships with suppliers based on mutual benefit, understanding, and trust. Such relationships can only flourish in an atmosphere of honesty, fairness, and high ethical standards. These prerequisites we are pledged to provide.

Introduction

Over the years, our corporation has gained a worldwide reputation as a manufacturer of quality products. Our suppliers have played a key role in our success, and their cooperation and dependability in providing quality materials, services, and ideas have contributed greatly.

We view the contribution of our suppliers in an atmosphere of mutual respect and understanding, in which honesty and fairness are ever-present guidelines. Some of the principles underlying this philosophy will be described in succeeding pages.

The overall purpose of this pamphlet is to introduce first-time (new) suppliers to us, and to supply them with enough information to begin the process. It is only through evaluating new suppliers and their products and services that we can remain competitive.

So, we welcome you and hope that this booklet is helpful in getting you started.

Fig. 6-2. A typical message to suppliers. Used with permission.

September
1989

Raytheon

Purchasing

Location

Guide

Martin J. Kane
Director-Procurement

Fig. 6-3. A sample page from a Raytheon purchasing location guide for suppliers. Used with permission.

ing that such a booklet is essential for developing mutually beneficial relations that extend far beyond the simple process of buying and selling.

Some corporate brochures for prospective suppliers include photographs, buying responsibilities, and direct-dial numbers for buyers. Northrop Corporation sends a monthly newsletter, *Small Business Purchasing*, to all suppliers—established or potential—on their mailing list. Pfizer sends out a brochure listing their product needs, plant locations, and telephone numbers. Some corporations send a supplier application form in response to queries from potential suppliers.

As a supplier who might be unfamiliar with the various corporate policies and procedures, getting a hold of a suppliers guide will enable you to give a better presentation once you've determined a need you can fulfill.

Some supplier guides address "end runs" around the purchasing department to technical staff. If they are not allowed, this is usually stated in the suppliers guide.

Corporations committed to using new vendors make suppliers guides readily available. The acid test is this: when you contact a corporation about providing products or services, you should immediately receive a supplier's guide.

Sometimes, after reviewing a supplier's guide you may decide that you do not have the products or services in need. Thus, you have saved yourself.

Many suppliers guides include a questionnaire (see Figs. 6-4 and 6-5). A questionnaire such as this is usually the first step in the procurement process, not merely a delaying tactic on the part of a corporation. These supplier application forms are important and should be filled out as completely and accurately as possible.

There is no advantage in beefing up your credentials on application forms. I've seen small suppliers who added 50 percent to their plant's square footage, "doubled" their number of employees, and added several years to how long they've been in business. These tactics never work in the long run. The purchasing agents with whom you will deal with have "seen it all." Your best chance is to maintain 100 percent honesty—really.

Many corporations such as Philip Morris and McDonnell Douglas produce directories of potential suppliers which are distributed to buyers throughout their corporation. Corporate supplier application forms provide the information for such directories as well as serving as a "ready reference" when a new source for supplies or new materials are required. The following are some of the items commonly found in suppliers guides:

- Business ethics policy.
- Small purchasing policy, including specific goals (if applicable).
- Items and services purchased by plant or buying center.
- Names, addresses, and phone numbers or specific purchasing managers, including their areas of responsibility.
- Best time of day or week to see buyers.
- Location of plants (if purchasing is decentralized).
- Background on company.
- What the corporation expects of its supplier and special qualifications required of supplier for specific products/services.
- Supplier questionnaire.

Not all corporations, however, have developed supplier guides and some that have don't distribute them in a timely manner. I've had trouble getting responses from Motorola, National Semiconductor, Bell and Howell, Abbott Laboratories, and Cummins Engine, for example.

Changes in the political, technological, social, and economic environments continue to alter the nature of the relationships between corporate purchasing departments and the suppliers seeking to do business with them. Nevertheless, as you research and call upon corporate giants, you'll find that the commitment to small suppliers among some is inspiring.

Why Should We Buy From You?

~ Have you presented a new idea to us lately?

~ What is your best idea to reduce our cost?

~ Do you have products or services that will increase our productivity? How?

~ Will your organization provide technical services to us?

~ Are your complete capabilities known to us? Are we using them?

~ Do you tell us promptly of new products or new ways to use existing ones?

~ What is your approach to quality? Do you know the consistency of the product you ship us—or just think you do—or assume it is okay unless you receive complaints?

~ What are you doing to improve consistency of your product quality?

~ Are you willing to certify your shipments to us as meeting quality standards?

~ Have you established a record of "delivery reliability" with us?

~ Is every shipment of your product within agreed-to tolerances, properly packaged, and marked with a code number, with the exact count, and shipped to the proper destination?

~ Do you always ship only the quantity ordered? (No overage unless within the agreed-to-size.)

~ Do you always ship on the specified date, and not before, unless the purchase order permits early shipment?

~ Do you always ship as instructed by us?

~ What specific ideas can you offer to minimize transportation costs on items we buy from you?

~ Will you hold prices longer for more business?

~ Terms are a part of price. We pay on time. Are your quoted prices on the basis of our prompt payment?

~ Have you developed a "Volume Discount" program with us?
Do you participate in our "Committed Stock" program?

~ Are you interested in consignment inventory on or near our premises?

~ Vendor stocking, on your premises, might offer opportunities for additional volume.

~ Review your lead time requirements with us. Shorter lead times might give you a competitive advantage.

Fig. 6-4. Corporate purchasing department vendor questions.

VENDOR QUESTIONNAIRE

Your company's name _____

Address _____ Phone (___)_____

City _____ State _____ Zip _____

Names of principals and partners _____
_____

Contact person and title _____

Describe type of goods or services provided (list SIC numbers if known)
_____
_____

Gross annual sales $_____ Number of employees _____

Years in business _____

_____ Sole proprietorship _____ Partnership _____ Corporation

Is the company a manufacturers' representative? _____ Yes _____ No

(If yes, list product lines carried) _____
_____
_____

Geographic service area _____

Ownership: (1) U.S. citizens? _____ Yes _____ No

           If no, permanent U.S. visas? _____

           (2) 51% minority owned? _____ Yes _____ No

Are you presently doing business with us? _____ Yes _____ No

Have you done so in the past? _____ (If yes, please complete the following.)

Division, Facility, City	Buyer's Name and Phone	Specific Product or Service
_____	_____	_____
_____	_____	_____
_____	_____	_____

Please list three company credit references:

Company Name	Contact Person	Address and Phone
_____	_____	_____
_____	_____	_____
_____	_____	_____

Please list three of your major clients:

Company Name	Contact Person	Address and Phone	Specific Product or Service
_____	_____	_____	_____
_____	_____	_____	_____
_____	_____	_____	_____

Give any other information you feel pertinent _____
_____

Submitted by (name): _____ Title _____ Date _____

Fig. 6-5. A vendor questionnaire.

7

Understanding the corporate purchasing psyche

PURCHASING AGENTS HAVE A GREAT DEAL MORE RESPONSIBILITIES than most suppliers realize. For example, purchasing agents routinely have the responsibility for:

- Evaluating suppliers
- Identifying, selecting, and developing new suppliers
- Scheduling purchases
- Scheduling deliveries
- Negotiating contracts
- Specifying mode of inbound shipments
- Controlling inventories
- Managing value analysis activities
- Determining whether to make or buy a component
- Deciding to lease versus purchase
- Visiting plant cites to evaluate suppliers (12 or more visits per year)

Increasingly, corporate representatives are visiting suppliers plants to gain a greater understanding of the suppliers operations.

PURCHASING AGENT

Pharmaceutical Inc., a leading manufacturer and distributor of generic pharmaceuticals is currently looking for a Purchasing Agent—Pharmaceuticals.

Reporting to the Vice-President of Operations, this newly designed function will be responsible for negotiating price and delivery schedules with our vendors, completing acquisition cost analysis, recommending alternative sources of supply, interfacing with internal marketing/manufacturing personnel to develop programs, meeting with customers/regulatory officials on an ad-hoc basis and providing quality assurance support for pharmaceuticals procured from outside vendors.

The candidate should be a R.Ph. with 2-5 years' pharmaceutical buying experience in a wholesale, retail or hospital environment. Strong written and communication skills are required as well as superior analytical talents and familiarity with mainframe and personal computer based data processing systems.

We offer an excellent salary and benefit package including medical, dental, profit sharing and bonus opportunities. Please send resume including salary history to:

Fig. 7-1. A classified advertisement for a purchasing agent.

The survey form in Fig. 7-1 is representative of that used by larger companies to evaluate potential suppliers.

Many purchasing agents have responsibility for specifying the mode or carrier for outbound shipments and for managing purchasing activities for other locations. Also, the purchasing agent often has the authority to reverse or change suppliers.

An occupation in transition

The more you know about purchasing management at major corporations, the better your chances will be for marketing success. Since World War II, purchasing has moved from the status of little more than a clerical function to a full-fledged position of the corporate management team. One of the many reasons why purchasing departments are growing in importance within major corporations is that, over the last several years, purchased goods and services are accounting for a growing share of the cost of goods produced.

Corporate purchasing departments today are staffed with well educated, well trained, and broadly experienced professionals. A *Purchasing World* study of professional purchasing based on responses from more than 1,300 readers selected at random shows that the typical reader is an educated, experienced decision-maker who has wide-ranging responsibilities and authority. According to the findings, the typical *Purchasing World* reader:

- Attended college, and about 10 percent of the respondents hold advanced degrees. The major field of study mentioned most often is business administration. A lesser number majored in engineering or liberal arts.

- Has about a dozen years experience in the purchasing function. About half of the respondents have been in purchasing for more than 10 years.

- Has not spent all of his or her business career in purchasing. Other work cited included production, inventory control, management, and sales and marketing.

- Is a member of company-wide committees, most often those concerned with cost reduction, standardization, and product design.

Continuous professional upgrade

Large corporations are pushing to upgrade the purchasing function even further. Purchasing involvement in corporate affairs is expanding, and the professional purchaser is now expected to apply innovative contracting and management methods, as well as have the ability to sell new ideas. Many corporations, such as Corning Glass Works and General Electric, have a vice president of purchasing.

Purchasing is getting more involved in such areas as corporate strategy and long-range planning; long-term agreements with major suppliers in different parts of the world; research and negotiation on critical materials to assure continuity of supply; major studies on make or buy; and close coordination with suppliers and user departments on significant quality problems. In the early 1990s, the majority of corporate purchasing departments will have additional responsibilities in the areas of packaging study and design review.

The purchasing professional has to distinguish between the strategic and tactical responsibilities of his department. The tactical job—placing orders, expediting, working with material control, checking vendor performance—is only half the job. The other half is the strategic efforts of long-range planning, forecasting, maintaining engineering interface, negotiating major contracts, and setting goals and objectives. One company, Boise Cascade, made an all out effort to involve purchasing in all of the functions at their origin.

The vice president for procurement at a major computer manufacturer had this to say about procurement professionals, ''We're looking for the MBA, the higher-level person. But if you hire those persons, you've got to challenge them.'' Specifically, this executive wants to upgrade salaries and job classifications and institute new ways to measure buyers' performances. ''I want to develop some kind of measurement program that can tell me what a buyer is doing from a professional point of view,'' he explains. ''We're looking at how they work with their peers at other organizations, with senior management, and with people they supervise, and how far they go to get the best prices, and how professionally they do it.'' At many corporations, purchasing professionals also:

- have dozens of decision-making responsibilities, from selection and evaluation of suppliers through control of inventories to choosing the mode or carrier for outbound and inbound shipments;

- spend more than $70 million a year for equipment, supplies, and services. One-quarter of the respondents spend more than $200 million annually;

- work closely with other key functions, primarily production, top management, and finance.

In some corporations, purchasing departments are responsible for handling such expenses as corporate travel, temporary office helpers, telecommunications services, trainers and consultants, security services and devices, and a host of other functions that, just five years ago, would have been out of the question for a purchasing agent to handle.

The certified purchasing manager

As with other professions, purchasing managers have accredited programs they can master that designates their professionalism and outstanding abilities. Several times throughout the calendar year, the National Association of Purchasing Management conducts a nationwide examination of purchasing professionals at more than 130 test locations throughout the United States. The examination consists of four modules including the:

1. purchasing function;
2. administrative function;
3. organizational function; and
4. continuing education function.

The exam generally takes all day. Total fees (1990) to take the four modules are $160 for members and $240 for allied associate members. More than 2,500 individuals took the most recent examination offered.

When you encounter a purchasing professional with a CPM after his or her name, you can be assured that he is a senior member of his profession who has demonstrated a mastery of fundamental skills and who has obtained an advanced level of awareness and experience within the profession.

High risk, high reward

There is an evolution toward more entrepreneurial leadership—more decision-making—closer to the everyday operating level. Chief executive officers are looking for purchasing types who have a broad understanding of their own companies' long-range strategies, an acute awareness of how purchasing can contribute to those strategies, plus the individual, professional ability to do it. Such is the case at Xerox, Eaton, and Pillsbury, among many other corporations.

The intense, expert, and comprehensive evaluation of suppliers continues to be a prime responsibility, however. In the environment of the 1990s, says the purchasing vice-president of a top chemical producer, purchasing's charter means, "more analysis, more study, more detail. You have to probe more deeply into all suppliers' qualifications. Purchasing agents need all of the information they can get to evaluate suppliers and make decisions as to whom they want to do business with." At Anheuser-Busch, purchasing personnel are expected to know the economics of supplying industries and to be aware of supplier capabilities and production problems.

At still other major corporations, purchasing officials are playing a bigger role in new product development. At a major aerospace corporation, the purchasing staff was restructured. The goal, says the new vice president for materials management, who spearheaded the initiative, was to "make our people professional managers of external manufacturing."

The "fit" that fits

Major corporations choose their vendors and suppliers with care to afford a good "fit" of products and processes. Life-of-the programcontracts and corporate-sponsored vendor training signal an era in which supplier dependability is an element upon which purchasing departments rely.

Supplier performance, however, in all aspects, comes through as purchasing's major concern today. Key performance factors include:

- Quality of purchased items
- Lead times
- Communication between supplier and buyer
- Supplier representatives' level of knowledge and technical expertise.

Of these factors, as discussed in chapter 1, *demonstrated* quality and reliability are by far the most important. In the past, cost reduction might have been the overriding concern for many corporate purchasing managers, but no longer. At an annual conference of the National Association of Purchasing Management, this message came through loud and clear. One speaker, a vice president for a leading international telecommunications corporation, said, "If you don't demand the best from your suppliers, your company won't end up with the best product."

Not all purchasing professionals are alike. One buyer might attempt to negotiate with a preferred supplier for a better price and terms before making a final selection. Another might select a single supplier or a few suppliers. Many buyers prefer multiple sources of supply, however, so that they will not be totally dependent on one supplier in case something goes wrong. In this case, they usually compare the prices and performance of the various suppliers.

Understanding how the world of the purchasing professional works is an important step on the road to marketing success with large corporations. If you can put yourself in the purchasing manager's shoes, the trip can be a lot easier than you might expect.

Understanding the purchasing structure

Let's examine the typical hierarchy of a corporate purchasing department according to the National Association of Purchasing Management.

Vice president or director of purchasing   The vice president or director of purchasing is often on par with other corporate VP's in marketing, administration, plant and operations, finance, and international divisions. This is the top purchasing position, primarily an administrator's role.

The head of a purchasing department, regardless of the title, is a member of the management team in the company. He/she has a multitude of major responsibilities and policies to supervise and administer. To reach the top positions, it is necessary to progress through the lower positions within the department.

Purchasing manager   The purchasing manager's duties are assigned depending on the level of management to which he/she is assigned. In most companies, the purchasing manager functions at two levels: He is doing some buying and, at the same time, supervising the buying activities of subordinates. See Fig. 7-1. In his capacity as supervisor to buyers and assistant purchasing managers, the manager is responsible for their training and development.

Procurement engineer   The duties of a procurement engineer are to analyze technical data, design preliminary specifications, and appraise manufacturing limitations, suppliers facilities, and the availability of materials and equipment. The procurement engineer consults with engineering personnel to establish performance criteria and construction and test specifications.

The procurement engineer investigates equipment manufacturers and interviews supplier representatives regarding specifications, costs, inspection, and other considerations. The procurement engineer arranges and participates in conferences between suppliers and engineers, purchasers, inspectors, and others to facilitate material inspection, substitution, standardization, rework, salvage, utilization, and economical procurement of equipment.

Purchasing analyst   The duties of a purchasing analyst are to compile and analyze statistical data to determine the feasibility of buying products, to establish price objectives for contract transactions, and to keep abreast of price trends and manufacturing processes. The analyst obtains data for cost analysis studies, confers with suppliers, and analyses suppliers' operations to determine factors that affect prices. See Fig. 7-2.

Expediter   The duties of an expediter largely depend upon the method of expediting and the degree of expediting employed. The expediter's job is either to speed up delivery from suppliers or to see that delivery commitments made by suppliers are adhered to.

In many companies, the job of the expediter is basically clerical in nature and involves the maintenance of an adequate set of tickler files and the follow-up of purchase orders to secure acceptances of the order and delivery data promises. In some companies, especially during periods of short supply, the job might also include field expediting. This might involve direct contact with suppliers at their plants. An expediter is exposed to almost all categories of purchases made by her company.

Traffic manager   A traffic manager is occasionally assigned

American Purchasing Society

IMPROVE PROFITS THROUGH

Modern Principles of Purchasing

A two day, four session seminar

Modern Principles of Purchasing is a two day concentrated course for anyone wanting an overall view of modern purchasing. The program is divided into four sessions which may be taken separately or in total.

The entire program is designed for either new buyers or purchasing managers with many years of experience who would like to review the fundamentals as well as learn about sophisticated purchasing practices. It is also excellent for general managers and others who supervise purchasing and who would like to have a better understanding of the total function. Every participant in the two day program will learn the thirteen essential do's and don'ts of good purchasing.

Session 1 is an introduction to the purchasing process and should be of most interest to new buyers and those who would like an overview of the purchasing process. Sesssion 2 covers the elements of business law that relate to purchasing transactions. You will learn what clauses you must use on a purchase order or in a purchase contract to protect your company's interest.

Session 3 gives you the various methods and strategies that are used in negotiating for products and services. Session 4 gives the purchasing manager or would be purchasing manager the know-how to manage the department efficiently and profitably.

The most common purchasing problems and their solutions will be discussed. All participants are encouraged to bring their purchasing problems for solution.

Session 1: PURCHASING DYNAMICS
- What you must know about the purchasing process.
- How to satisfy the requisitioner.
- How purchasing interacts with all departments.
- What you need to document and how to do it.
- How to reduce paperwork and save time.
- How to find and evaluate sources.
- How to get the quality you want.
- When you should use differet types of orders.
- How to get delivery when you need it.
- What you need to know about prices and cost.
- How you can contribute most to company profits.
- How you can be rated as a purchasing professional.

Session 2: WHAT YOU NEED TO KNOW ABOUT PURCHASING LAW
- Your legal responsibility as a buyer or purchasing agent.
- Why you should determine a salespersons authority.
- Why non-purchasing personnel should not place orders.
- What you must know about purchase orders and contracts.
- The differences between oral and written contracts.
- When a bid or offer is binding.
- The importance of the UCC to the buyer.
- What terms should be included with every order.
- When you can and cannot cancel an order.
- The types of warranties and how you can protect yourself.
- What you must know about the anti-trust laws.
- What you must know about patents before you buy.

Session 3: HOW TO NEGOTIATE FOR PURCHASING
- Who negotiates.
- How much you can obtain.
- What is negotiable.
- When you should negotiate.
- Methods of negotiating and which to use.
- How to prepare for negotiation.
- How to set objectives.
- Strategies used by buyers and sellers.
- Timing considerations for negotiating.
- Powerful tools and techniques to use.
- Why negotiations fail.
- How to renegotiate a contract.

Session 4: MANAGING PURCHASING TO IMPROVE COMPANY PERFORMANCE
- What you need to know about purchasing budgets.
- How to analyze your workload and staff your department.
- How you select qualified purchasing personnel.
- How to evaluate purchasing performance.
- How you should plan purchasing activities.
- Why you should have policy and procedure manuals.
- Which policies to include.
- How to use value analysis.
- Using purchasing staff for analyses and forecasting.
- How to maximize the use of the computer.
- The major purchasing problems and how to solve them.
- Seven common purchasing mistakes

Fig. 7-2. A typical American Purchasing Society seminar offering.

as a subdivision of the purchasing department. Traffic management deals primarily with the problems inherent in securing delivery of the purchased materials.

Buyer   A buyer might perform one or more of the following duties in purchasing a widely diversified group of raw materials, components, or finished parts, such as chemicals, paper and board, office equipment and supplies, printing, electronics equipment and supplies, building supplies, metals, pipe and fittings, and various services, etc. To accomplish this, the buyer:

1. Edits requisitions and confers with departments regarding requirements, specifications, quantity, quality of merchandise, and delivery requirements. Recommends substitutes where savings and improved delivery will result.

2. Solicits and analyzes quotations for new or nonstandard items. Negotiates with suppliers to obtain most favorable terms of purchase. Recommends or approves awarding of contracts or purchase orders, ensuring that all purchases comply with government regulations and accepted trade practices.

3. Interviews suppliers and their representatives personally, and maintains close contact by correspondence and plant visits.

4. Arranges with subcontractors to fabricate special equipment from company blueprints. Checks blueprints for errors and completeness of information so that the supplier can comply with special requirements.

5. Carries out necessary follow-up and expediting activities to ensure delivery as required by production schedules.

6. Serves in an advisory capacity to assist other departments to obtain proper specifications, quotations, delivery terms, and cost.

7. Might examine and approve all invoices covering purchase orders placed.

8. Handles adjustments with suppliers involving replacement of materials not conforming to purchase specifications, return of materials declared surplus as a result of engineering changes, cancellation of orders, etc., prepares shipping orders and ensures that appropriate credit is received.

9. Maintains an appropriate file of catalogs, price lists, etc., to be available for use of departments to assist them in obtaining the latest information with reference to new products.

In many large corporations, the duties of buyers call for very highly-trained specialists who have a narrow range of commodities which they will buy. According to the National Association of Purchasing Management, there could be several categories of buying, including general products construction, production materials and components, raw materials and commodities, and governmental and institutional buying.

Classifying corporate buyers

There are all types of buyers in large corporations but most purchasing professionals can be categorized into one of the following five groups:

1. *General products buyer.* This type of buying is characterized by the wide range of materials, generally of low unit value, and might include maintenance materials, tools, spare parts, and operating supplies. This sort of assignment is likely to be the first buying assignment given to the novice buyer in a larger company. Because of the wide range of experiences this position offers, it provides an ideal training ground for young professionals in purchasing.

2. *Construction buyer.* This type of buying is at the opposite extreme in terms of the responsibilities involved. A construction buyer handles the negotiations for buildings and facilities as well as the procurement of major items of equipment. This type of buying position is likely to be found only in large companies. In smaller companies, construction and equipment buying is handled by the head of the purchasing department or even by the head of the company.

   In general, personnel assigned to this type of buying are moved from other categories of buyers. This is not the beginner's assignment. Almost universally, companies would require a college education for this type of buying. In many cases, the assignment goes to an engineering graduate.

3. *Production materials or components buyer.* This type of buying covers those items purchased to the user's specifications and design for incorporation into the final product. A materials or components buyer must have a wide knowledge of processing and manufacturing techniques. In many instances, companies will assign subcontracting negotiations to this buyer.

4. *Raw material or commodity buyer.* Buyers in this category are generally specialists. In many cases, the buyer is a member of the executive group of the company, particularly where basic raw material constitutes a substantial portion of the total purchases of the company. Examples might be grain buying by flour millers and hides buying by a tannery. In many companies, the volume of purchases of the basic raw material is so great that no other buying is assigned to this buyer. An example would be the coal buyer for a large electric utility.

   Successful raw material or commodity buyers must have the skill and ability to study and forecast market trends and general business conditions. This position calls for a college graduate in either a technical or business field. The ideal qualifications for this type of buying is an undergraduate technical degree and a master's degree in business administration.

5. *Governmental and institutional buying:* Works much the same as industrial purchasing.

Understanding purchasing departments

There are three basic categories into which industrial purchasing departments themselves can be organized:

1. *Centralized.* This is usually one large purchasing department at corporate headquarters that buys for all plants and facilities.

2. *Semi-centralized.* This type of purchasing department is usually arranged where the headquarters' purchasing department purchases all big-ticket items for the corporation and each plant purchases its own small or specialized items. In this case, individual plants might be limited by total dollars spent with approval needed from headquarters for any purchases over the limit.

3. *Decentralized.* Decentralized purchasing means each plant or facility purchases all of its materials, equipment, and services. A headquarters purchasing department might oversee individual locations but the amount of the influence they have varies with each corporation. Most companies maintain a decentralized purchasing system.

Getting the inside word

New business prospecting is the most difficult and arduous part of sales, but it can also be the most rewarding. Begin by canvassing buyers and customers with whom you have previously done business. Ask them for names of buyers representing large firms you want to solicit. A referral is a more personal approach and eliminates some of the rigors involved in prospecting. Purchasing agents, for example, can put you in touch with key engineers and technicians (see chapter 8) who generate job requirements.

Having inside information on purchasing opportunities is the key to staying ahead of the competition. Surprisingly, the inside information you want is not hidden away in corporate files. It is readily available at nominal cost, in the form of purchasing magazines, journals, and handbooks. See Fig. 7-3.

Purchasing periodicals

The following is a list of the leading trade periodicals read by purchasing managers. Consequently, you should be reading them too, and as a purchaser yourself, you qualify for a free subscription to those publications offered at no charge. See Fig. 7-4.

- *Distribution* (monthly), Chilton Company, Chilton Way, Radnor, PA 19089.

- *Industrial Distribution* (monthly), Cahners Publishing Company, 275 Washington Street, Newton, MA 02158-1611.

- *Industry Week* (weekly), Penton, IPC, 1100 Superior Avenue, Cleveland, OH 44114.

- *Professional Purchasing* (monthly), American Purchasing Society, 11910 Oak Trail Way, Port Richey, FL 34668.

- *Purchasing* (biweekly), Cahners Publishing, 275 Washington Street, Newton, MA 02158-1611.

- *Purchasing Management* (monthly), 14 North 7th Street, St. Cloud, MN 56301.

- *Purchasing Management* (bimonthly), Clifford/Elliot & Associates, 277 Lakeshore Road East, #209, P.O. Box 247, Oakville Ontario L6J 6J3.

- *Purchasing World* (monthly), Huebcore Communications, Inc., 29,100 Aurora Road, Solon, OH 44139.

These publications contain articles with inside information directed towards purchasing professionals. You will find material

Professional Books, Reprints, & Services Available From Purchasing Magazine

Books

How Industry Buys — Part I	$15.00
How Industry Buys — Part II	25.00
Just-In-Time/USA	15.00
How To Buy Software	25.00
Computers in Purchasing Handbook	32.50
Systems Purchasing Handbook	22.50
Metals Sourcing Guide	49.00
Buying Quality	25.00
A Guide to Purchasing Law	30.00
Value Analysis Handbook	40.00
How Industry Buys for the Office	19.00
PC Basics for Buyers	35.00
Transportation Sourcing Guide	49.00

Reprints

Computers in Purchasing (reprint) Part 1-13	6.00
Computers in Purchasing (reprint) Part 14-26	6.00
How your job is changing and what it means	2.00

Services

Buying Strategy Forecast (26 issues)	225.00
Transaction Pricing Service (quarterly update of prices)	
Metals (per year)	125.00
Paper and paperboard (per year)	125.00
Chemicals (per year)	125.00
Plastics (per year)	125.00
Wood products (per year)	125.00
All five groups (per year)	600.00

Purchasing Magazine

Price includes shipping. For your copies or subscriptions, send payments to:
Purchasing Magazine's Books and Reprints, P.O. Box 497
Newton Branch, Boston, MA 02258.

Fig. 7-3. Advertisement for Purchasing *books and reprints. Printed with permission.*

Purchasing

Free Subscription/Change of Address Form

Please answer all questions, **sign and date the card.**
Incomplete forms cannot be processed or acknowledged.
The publisher reserves the right to serve only those individuals who meet the publication qualifications.

PUR-473

A **Please send/continue to send free copies of Purchasing magazine (and Directories):** Yes ☐ No ☐

▶**X**_____
　YOUR SIGNATURE (REQUIRED)　　　　　　　date

_____
Your name (please print)

_____
Title (please print)　　　( )_____
　　　　　　　　　　　business phone

B **For change of address—Please make changes on label and affix below.**

┌─── **Please Affix Label Within This Box** ───┐

company name

division　　　　　　　department

mailing address

city　　　　　　state　　　zip code
└─────────────────────────────┘

C **Is the above your home address?** Yes ☐ No ☐

D **If your title is not a purchasing title, is purchasing your function?** 1 ☐ Yes　2 ☐ No

E **Number of purchasing professionals with buying authority at this location. (Check 1 box)**

3 ☐ 1-2　4 ☐ 3-5　5 ☐ 6-9　6 ☐ 10-19
7 ☐ 20-49　8 ☐ 50-99　9 ☐ 100+

F **What is your level of authority? (Check 1 box)**

10 ☐ I am primarily a manager
11 ☐ I have some management authority
12 ☐ I have a staff position

G **Name and title of the individual to whom the Purchasing department reports:**

13/_____　14/_____
　　name　　　　　　　　　　　title

H **Approximate number of employees at this location (Check 1 box)**

15 ☐ 1000+　17 ☐ 500-999　19 ☐ 250-499
16 ☐ 100-249　18 ☐ 50-99　20 ☐ 20-49　21 ☐ 1-19

J **What is the primary end product manufactured (or service performed) at this location? (Be specific)**

_____

If this is a manufacturing company and there is no manufacturing at this location, check if:

25 ☐ Central or District Administrative Office
26 ☐ Research Laboratory　28 ☐ Warehouse
27 ☐ Sales Office　29 ☐ Other

Fig. 7-4. A Purchasing subscription form.

Please do not write above this line.

K 1. In the performance of my job, I buy or supervise the buying of the following products or services: (check all that apply)
2. Please also check if you buy some or all the products through a distributor:

Buy or super-vise the buying of:	Buy some or all through distri-butors	(Check one or both)
30 ☐	53 ☐	Assembly Components
31 ☐	54 ☐	Chemicals
32 ☐	55 ☐	Electronic components, Equipment and supplies
33 ☐	56 ☐	Electrical equipment and supplies (motors, switches, batteries)
34 ☐	57 ☐	Hydraulic, pneumatic & fluidic equipment & supplies (hose pumps compressors)
35 ☐	58 ☐	Instruments (measuring, metering and recording)
36 ☐	59 ☐	Lubricants & other petroleum products
37 ☐	60 ☐	Materials handling equipment and supplies (trucks, conveyors, hoists)
38 ☐	61 ☐	Mechanical parts (stampings, springs, forgings)
39 ☐	62 ☐	Non-ferrous metals (aluminum, brass)
40 ☐	63 ☐	Non-metallic materials except chemicals, petroleum and plastic products (rubber, glass)
41 ☐	64 ☐	Computers, peripherals, software
42 ☐	65 ☐	Office/business machines and equipment
43 ☐	66 ☐	Furniture, filing systems office
44 ☐	67 ☐	Office and business supplies
45 ☐	68 ☐	Packaging (cartons, labeling, strapping)
46 ☐	69 ☐	Plant & personnel health or safety equipment & supplies (clothing, towels, eyewear)
47 ☐	70 ☐	Plant services & facilities (lighting, manual valves, energy)
48 ☐	71 ☐	Plastics (materials, parts, resins)
49 ☐	72 ☐	Power transmission products (V-belts, gears, bearings)
50 ☐	73 ☐	Production equipment (power tools, cutting tools, welding)
51 ☐	74 ☐	Steel and other ferrous metals
52 ☐	75 ☐	Other (please describe) 76 _____

77 ☐ I have no responsibility to buy or supervise the buying of any of the products or services listed above.

78 ☐ Do not buy through distributors

L In the performance of my job, I specify, recommend, approve or purchase the following transportation services: (Check all that apply)

80 ☐ Motor freight　　83 ☐ Package express service
81 ☐ Rail carriers　　84 ☐ International transportation
82 ☐ Air freight　　85 ☐ Other transportation services
　　　　　　　　86 ☐ None of the above

M Check the publications below that you personally receive.

90 ☐ Business Week　　93 ☐ Metalworking News
91 ☐ Industry Week　　94 ☐ NED
92 ☐ Purchasing World
　　　95 ☐ None of the above

on how suppliers are found, vendor evaluations, negotiation tactics, purchasing law, and other purchasing management tips.

The information and insights in these periodicals is of very high quality. *Any* would-be supplier to large corporations would gain immediate benefit by reading them. Many issues spotlight purchasing programs and people at major corporations. Over the past few years, for example, *Purchasing* and *Purchasing World* have ran in-depth features on Chrysler, Pacific Bell, Phillips Petroleum, Parker Hannifin, Intel, Xerox, General Motors, Deere & Company, and many other large corporations. These articles, a veritable ''Who's Who'' of corporate purchasing executives, can be a potential gold mine of marketing contacts.

There are also regional purchasing periodicals published by affiliates of the National Association of Purchasing Management, as well as independently operated periodicals that can help you keep current on issues and opportunities closer to home. Titles and addresses of regional publications can be found in Appendix A.

An entire roster of books, reprints, and information services is available from *Purchasing Management*. These resources cover the world of purchasing. Here are just some of the topics of interest to the suppliers.

- How costs are determined.
- Purchasing ethics.
- How Just-in-Time programs work in the United States.
- Negotiating sole-source items.
- How to make suppliers justify cost increases.
- How industry buys for the office.
- Checking the legal angle before buying.
- Improving buyer-seller relationships.
- Checking supplier financial reports.
- How to use value analysis.
- A look at worldwide purchasing.
- How suppliers rate purchasers.
- How to work more effectively with suppliers.

A particularly handy guide is *How Industry Buys,* a compilation of how progressive corporations do their buying. Suppliers who understand corporate purchasing from the inside out have the best chance of sustained success. Accelerate your understanding by taking time to read what the purchasing industry itself has to offer.

Purchasing professionals are continuously upgrading their knowledge and skills through specialized seminars and training programs. The following are some examples of popular programs and sponsors:

Basic Blueprint Reading for Buyers, Boston. Sponsor: Nahabit & Associates, Inc., 25239 via Tanara, Valencia, CA

Effective Negotiating, Indianapolis. Sponsor: Karrass, 1633 Stanford St., Santa Monica, CA 90404

Legal Aspects of Purchasing, Chicago. Sponsor: American Management Association, P.O. Box 319, Saranac Lake, NY 12983

Negotiating in a JIT Environment, Ft. Lauderdale. Sponsor: National Association of Purchasing Management, 2055 East Centennial Circle, P.O. Box 22160, Tempe, AZ 85285

Purchasing in the 1990s, Wisconsin. Sponsor: Management Institute, The School of Business, University of Wisconsin—Madison, 432 N. Lake St., Madison, WI 53706

Supplier Certification, Tempe, AZ. Sponsor: National Association of Purchasing Management, 2055 East Centennial Circle, P.O. Box 22160, Tempe, AZ 85285

Time Management and Paperwork Reduction in Purchasing, Secaucus, NJ. Sponsor: National Association of Purchasing Management, 2055 East Centennial Circle, P.O. Box 22160, Tempe, AZ 85285

Modern Principles of Purchasing, Chicago. Sponsor: American Purchasing Society, 11910-B Oak Trail Way, Port Richey, FL 34668 (see seminar description)

Local "inside" information

It is important not to overlook local sources of information such as the chamber of commerce, Rotarians, Kiawanis, and other civic clubs that generally have directories of members and their business affiliations. Try to join one of these clubs or at least be invited to one or several of their meetings. These clubs schedule weekly or monthly meetings that provide excellent opportunities to meet prospects and arrange for new business presentations on a less formal basis.

Some medium and large size cities have local purchasing associations for buyers that usually schedule weekly or monthly luncheons. Such functions, if they are open to outside professionals, offer good opportunities to meet with local buyers. Also, be on the lookout for directories of corporate purchasers in your region.

Get your company's name on as many pertinent corporate

mailing lists as possible. Many municipal and state business development offices provide names of firms locating in new areas by making announcements through their mailing lists.

Consider the professionals you work with each day, often, they can provide valuable leads. Check with your insurance salesman for the names of executives of large firms in your area. Lawyers, stockbrokers, and consultants all can be useful in gaining inside information.

You and your company *can* get very close to the people who manage the business of buying goods and services for the large corporation. Like any successful business venture, however, it takes planning and persistence.

8

Calling on corporations

TO EFFECTIVELY CALL ON CORPORATE GIANTS, YOU MUST UNDERTAKE a series of strategic steps. The most critical being your meeting with the purchasing manager of other corporate representative. At this one-on-one meeting you can score big or watch a marketing opportunity fall apart. It is important to send experienced, mature sales representatives, particularly when dealing with the purchasing agents who have responsibilities for the purchase of millions of dollars of goods and services each year. In this chapter, we'll focus on elements for successfully calling on purchasing agents, including:

- Preparation
- Professionalism
- Presentation
- Proof
- Performance

Preparation

Establishing productive business relationships with new customers is a challenging task. For purchasing managers at most large corporations, time is a valuable commodity and their first impressions of potential suppliers are critical. The key to most triumphant presentations is advance preparation. By now, you should have all the pertinent information you need about the prospect (see chapter 6), including annual and quarterly corporate reports, product and service pamphlets, supplier guides, other company brochures, and industry information. Be sure to review them carefully so that when you're making your presentation late, you can refer to some of these items directly.

Next, identify and define your prospective buyer's needs—to the extent possible—before shaping your presentation. Is the prospect coming off a profitable quarter and looking to expand? Is he seeking to reduce inventories and costs? Is just-in-time delivery preferable? What is the buyer's highest priority at this time—quality upgrades? Low price?

Many large corporations designate certain days of the week on which buyers are available for appointments. It is important to state in your letter or phone call that you intend to make a new business presentation and would welcome any other company personnel to attend. Suggest a time and date for a meeting. Include with your letter a brochure, pamphlet, or other printed materials that favorably reflect your firm's capabilities.

If you will be calling, offer to mail some of your promotional materials. In fact, many buyers will immediately ask for these. When phoning to make an appointment, expect to have to make several calls and to spend time on hold. Even if you've researched this prospect to a tee, you're still likely to be put on hold, and it won't help to convey irritation once you reach the right party. View these calls as an opportunity to describe your company and your product or service to a potential buyer-one of many steps that will be needed in marketing your products or services. It is also useful to keep a record of contact names. The annual report or suppliers guide are good places to note them because you might be talking with these people again.

You might want to have a staff person handle the preliminary steps and exploratory telephone calls. This will save you time in identifying and locating the right person. After the groundwork has been completed, you can then place the important marketing call to the appropriate purchasing agent.

To interest the potential buyer in your product or service, you must first set the stage for a face-to-face meeting. This allows you to make a strong business presentation. Specify the amount of time you would like the buyer to allocate for your presentation. Some buyers place strict time limitations on appointments and new business presentations. Choosing an odd amount of time might prove extremely effective. After all, how many purchasing agents are told "my presentation will require 17 minutes?" In any case, it is important to clarify how much time the purchasing agent will have to spend with you beforehand.

As the meeting time approaches, even more effort must be made in preparation. Most purchasing managers are well-educated and broadly experienced professionals. They are paid to be thorough, but they are also human and will respond positively to a professional presentation. The advertising and public relations manager of a Virginia-based development company advises meeting purchasing agents on their own level. "We want every contact we make to convey a high degree of professionalism, quality, and service. Our presentations are carefully tailored to the prospect." So practice—with your staff, in the mirror, or on a tape recorder so that each presentation is an "award-winning effort."

Much of your presentation should be devoted to reviewing annual reports or company literature. Read them until you are familiar with the corporation's recent history, present leadership, and future plans.

If you have previously called on a corporation, obviously, your preparation should also include a file review. Your past relationship with a corporation, if any, provides the foundation on which you will build a future contract. From your files, you might be reminded:

- how contact with the corporation began;
- to whom your correspondence has been addressed;
- to whom you have spoken on the phone.

Those vendors that review a corporation's literature in the corporate reception area greatly reduce their odds for success. It is no wonder when they don't understand the corporation's current needs and goals.

Professionalism

Naturally, the first meeting with a purchasing agent is usually accompanied by some anxiety. Confirm your appointment one day in advance by telephone. On meeting day, plan an early arrival to the plant or corporate headquarters. Use any extra time to collect your thoughts and to review your presentation, while you sit in your car or somewhere else outside the corporate gates. Make critical checks. Is your briefcase organized so that you can easily obtain any documents you need? Do you have a neat pad or notebook to use for jotting notes during the interview? These notes could later be used when a contract is being prepared.

Enter the meeting with confidence, enthusiasm, and drive, but never overpower a prospect. Dress for success, be well rested, and keep your mind clear of other business distractions. Arrive at least five minutes early. Inventor Richard Levy, who regularly sells to large companies, says ''The first several minutes, indeed seconds, of your encounter are crucial.'' We often form lasting impressions of someone based on our first impressions. Don't allow the first impression a purchasing agent has of you to be one of a scrambling, chaotic, disorganized person. Get there early and stay in stride.

Presentation

Unless invited to stay longer, your presentation should be brief but thorough. Mentally rehearse what you will say. Establish a common ground with your prospect. Some very brief small talk is a good icebreaker. Mention the name of one of your customers with whom you think the buyer might be familiar.

Consider using samples, an audiovisual aid such as pictures, or a simple slide presentation. If the purchasing manager has never seen your location or met your personnel, he might appreciate such an approach. The major focus of your presentation should be on how you can fulfill her buying needs. Because the buyer-supplier relationship is increasingly looked upon as a partnership, including a long-term relationship, demonstrate that you are a supplier of reputation. Your chief task is to leave no doubt in the purchasing manager's mind that you can deliver.

The ability to ask good questions is also helpful in presentations, in sales situations, and in dealing with people in general. The following checklist ensures that you turn a superior performance during your presentation:

- *Be clear about your objectives.* Are you trying to close a sale on a specific item on this initial call, or are you seeking to make a contact and crystallize the buyer's needs?

- *Articulate the potential matches* between the buyer's needs and your goods and services. Be precise and clear about these matches.

- *Emphasize quality* in your presentation. Generally speaking, quality goods and services are the highest priorities for purchasing managers. Give specific examples of your quality control procedures. Show how quality control results in reduced waste.

- *Focus on dependability.* Emphasize your commitment to timely and reliable delivery. Describe your warranty and liability protection benefits, if any. Mention how your dependability has helped other customers.

- *Highlight cost-competitiveness.* Be prepared to justify your costs and the prices you charge with specific data. A simple cost-value analysis on previous jobs should reveal cost-cutting factors and demonstrate your ability to minimize waste and rework.

- *Be specific about your contracting procedures.* Include a sample of your standard sales agreement, if appropriate.

- *Use visuals and other materials* to support your oral presentation. For example, graphs are an effective way to illustrate growth in sales revenues or increased production performance. Well-done brochures that describe your corporate capabilities lend an aura of professionalism to your business. However, there is no need to go overboard on audiovisuals.

- *Be positive, enthusiastic, and responsive* to the customer's wishes during the presentations. Be sensitive to the buyer's needs at all times; don't waste his/her time on topics about which no interest is indicated. Be prepared to answer questions during your presentations. Solicit additional questions at the end of your prepared remarks.

If possible, bring along one or two of your key employees who would be working on the prospective customer's account.

They can answer specific questions and help establish the rapport necessary for good customer relations.

Conclude your presentation by establishing the steps for future action. Will you get a price quotation to the buyer by a specific date? Will you invite the buyer to tour your facility? Or will you call within a week to follow-up the presentation? The mark of supersellers is follow up; the mark of the majority of would-be suppliers is lack of follow-up.

Gage whether the buyer is merely seeking bid quotes for a pricing decision or is exploring other purchasing issues as well. This will help you focus your remarks on his/her needs. Two final steps should be taken within a day or two of your actual presentation:

1. Assess your presentation. Create a "lessons learned" list of what went well in the presentation and what needs to be changed in future presentations.

2. Write a follow-up letter. The letter should thank the agent for meeting with you and identify what you plan to do next for him/her.

The first impression you create is, indeed, critical. Unless the customer is impressed with *you* personally and the company you represent, he/she might never follow-up the presentation with further qualification activities. And, as a result, he/she might never find out what a good product or service your company can deliver.

Proof

Although only a few words are needed in regard to proof, they are important ones. During your meeting with the purchasing manager, you must be prepared to *document* your company's ability to produce (see chapter 5). A brochure, folder, or capability statement that describes what you can do is helpful and can be bolstered by:

- letters of recommendation
- testimonials
- references
- notices of certification
- certified capability statements
- copies of recent awards

Performance

Performance relates not only to how you fulfill you contract, but also how you perform prior to the contract being drawn up. The notes you took during your meeting form the base of the outline for your follow-up letter. The letter should:

- review important points covered during the meeting;
- provide answers to any questions that required research; and
- confirm actions that were agreed upon.

When the purchasing agent receives your letter, he might remember the meeting and recognize that you are someone who follows through on details. Never promise more than you can deliver. If a purchasing agent begins to expect more than your company is capable of doing, let the truth be known; maintain your integrity. It is better to promise and deliver on a small or medium order than to over-promise on a large one and ruin your firm's reputation. You could lose a repeat customer as well.

Some—not many—purchasing manager's consciously use intimadation tactics. They may want to see how you handle yourself under pressure. Some simply may have very little time available. In either case, your preparation and professional follow through will give you a decided edge in handling tougher situations, and that may give you the edge on getting the contract. Use the checklist shown in Fig. 8-1 to ensure that you have covered every base.

Calling on technical personnel

An important and particularly effective strategy when calling on corporations, particularly if you offer a highly technical product or specialized service, is to bolster your presentation efforts by making contact with the engineering or technical personnel who generate the work requirements. Contacting technical personnel without going through the proper purchasing department channels could backfire, however, so use your best judgment.

Corporate purchasing policy

Virtually all corporations specify in writing that no personnel outside the purchasing department have authority to commit to purchasing material or services from a supplier. This ensures proper coordination of their policy and procedures in working with suppliers. Always ask for a copy of the corporate (see page 114A) sup-

Checklist for Calling on a Purchasing Agent

Preparation

1. Review the corporation's annual report, company newsletters, supplier guide, etc.
2. Identify and define prospective buyer's needs.
3. Phone or write for an appointment.
4. Plan a brief but thorough presentation.
5. Rehearse your presentation.

Professionalism

1. Confirm the appointment.
2. Arrive at the plant or office early and become comfortable.
3. Organize your briefcase, documents, and notebook or pad.
4. Check your appearance.
5. Arrive at the appropriate office five minutes early.

Presentation

1. Break the ice with a minimum amount of small talk.
2. Be positive, brisk, and brief.
3. Provide company brochures, etc.
4. Use samples or simple audio visual aids.
5. Listen attentively.
6. Be positive.
7. Take notes.

Proof

1. Provide documentation on your firm's capability.
2. Provide recent project descriptions your firm recently handled.

Performance and follow-up

1. Assess your presentation.
2. Use your meeting notes for a follow-up letter.
3. Write a follow-up letter immediately.
4. Prepare to repeat this cycle.

Fig. 8-1. A checklist can make your first meeting with a purchasing agent successful.

plier guide if they have one, and most do, which will explain the corporate purchasing philosophy, guidelines, and operating procedures.

Your first point of contact with the corporation should always be the appropriate purchasing department. If the corporation is decentralized, as a majority are, make an appointment with the appropriate plant or facility. Even if purchasing personnel are not technically oriented themselves, they will be able to help you identify needs within the corporation. Purchasing will have the final say regardless of what connections you make with the technical staff and could make things difficult for a supplier they feel is attempting an "end-run."

If the corporation has a small business supplier coordinator, go through this person for your initial contact. Ignoring the coordinator might mitigate your marketing effectiveness. It is the responsibility of the coordinator to ensure that suppliers have all the information they need to make a credible sales pitch. At corporations like Harris, FMC Corporation, and Zenith, you might be pleasantly surprised by the assistance provided by their small vendor coordinators. The small business vendor coordinator can help you gain access to key engineering and technical personnel.

Does it help to make your capabilities known to others not in purchasing? The director of administration services at Amtrak is responsible for writing and establishing supply specifications. Though he has no actual purchasing authority, he frequently receives brochures and capability statements from prospective suppliers. "I pass along everything I get to the appropriate purchasing people," he says. "However, I do read what suppliers send in, and if I happen to come across a particularly attractive package from a seemingly highly qualified supplier, I let purchasing know."

Discovering technical needs

There are ways to find out the technical needs of a corporation without directly asking or bypassing the purchasing department. Join appropriate local associations of engineers or other professionals and listen to their discussions. When you contact the purchasing department, you can say that you heard about a certain technical need through a social contact and you would like some advice on the proper channels to follow.

Another way to find out the specific needs of a corporation is to ask the purchasing staff member for an appointment to see the specifying engineer. This person is responsible for specific materials used on a job and will often recommend to the purchasing department that a certain supplier be used. In high technology areas especially, such "pre-selections" are often made very early in the procurement process.

In some cases the specifying engineer is assigned to the purchasing department. Asking to see her will show your interest in the project and, again your willingness to work with the purchasing department through the proper channels.

"Suppliers who take the initiative to analyze and evaluate needs and functions can uncover many opportunities for good payback,'' reported one procurement manager with an aircraft manufacturing company. Corporations appreciate, and often count on the input of suppliers for value engineering savings.

If you can find the names of the engineers on a particular project before you see the purchasing department, you will make a favorable impression for having done your homework and perhaps gain key inside information. You might want to call the switchboard and ask in advance for the name of an engineer on a specific project, while not actually speaking to the engineer until you have checked with the purchasing department.

Once you have cleared with the purchasing department and have an appointment with the engineering or technical people, all of the previously supplied suggestions on marketing, documentation, and presentations are applicable.

Play both against the middle

Purchasing and technical personnel are complimentary in function. As a supplier, you must satisfy the requirements of both to be successful. Use purchasing to identify general needs and to make appointments with the appropriate technical people. Impress the technical department with your capabilities and understanding of their needs. If you can demonstrate that you recognize the importance and function of each department, you might well end up with both departments on your side.

Appendix B contains a listing of the addresses of scores of purchasing departments of major U.S. corporations and non-manufacturing organizations, alphabetical by state. Remember, addresses and numbers change frequently, often by 20 percent every 12 months. Continual updating is a necessity!

9

Using trade shows as a marketing tool

ONE WAY TO GAIN MAXIMUM MARKETING LEVERAGE OF YOUR TIME AND resources is by exhibiting at trade shows. Trade shows are the sacred selling turf of corporate America. If something can be shown to prospective buyers or clients—even if only in a picture—there is probably an annual or semiannual trade show related to it. Trade shows are a major, fast-growing method for demonstrating products and services. They present key positioning opportunities for savvy vendors. They can be aimed at the general public, such as home product shows, or at dealers and sales representatives, such as ski resort shows targeted for travel agents.

If you think about the client base for your product or service, from the individual purchaser to the geographical distributor, more than likely, you'll find a trade show for that client base.

A growing number of suppliers have found that using trade shows as a marketing vehicle can provide an effective cost/benefit ratio. In fact, the cost per new customer by exhibiting at trade shows can be lower than many of the other traditional marketing vehicles you've probably tried, such as direct mail, yellow pages advertising, and long distance telemarketing.

Advantages

Trade shows themselves have become something of a phenomenon. Well over 1,500 exhibits and trade shows are held each year just in the United States. More than 20,000 association-based conventions and exhibitions are held annually, many of which are listed in the *Directory of Conventions*. Regardless of what you are offering, there's bound to be a trade show that's right for you.

Attending trade shows allows you to contact a large number of prospective buyers in a short time, as well as the opportunity to see potential competitors and the products/services they are offering. Trade shows can also provide ideas for new products, services, or methods of distribution.

Attending a show enables you to gain experience in dealing with prospective clients. This interaction can reveal areas of a presentation that need clarification, products/services that are desired from a prospective buyer, modifications that would enhance a product's demand, or the need to develop a completely new product/service to add to an existing line. Appendix C contains a list of directories you can use to find out more information on trade shows.

Exhibitors can quickly find an audience that is prepared to "talk business." Exhibiting at trade shows has both its advantages and disadvantages. One exhibiting supplier concluded that you can can meet "an awful lot of people in a short time," but if you're exhibiting at the wrong trade show or your marketing presentation needs polishing, you could end up wasting a lot of time and money.

Exhibiting

Being part of a trade show is not at all inexpensive, but when you realize how many interested people you will see face-to-face in a short time, especially compared to the time it would take to personally visit each, the cost becomes a real bargain. Because you will get maximum exposure by presenting your business at a trade show, however, you can't skimp. You need plenty of trained staff on hand to demonstrate your wares, hand out brochures and other literature that explains your business and answers commonly asked questions.

Other costs include registration and space rental, and you need to either rent or ship a booth to set up in your space. You also need healthy amounts of written product or service information as hand-outs, and either a demonstration model or a film or video that visually depicts what you are selling.

In addition to these obvious costs, there are substantial costs in terms of your time and the time of your staff, not just during the trade show itself but in the planning and follow-up processes.

The cost of exhibiting can range anywhere from $800 to $1,400 for a local or a small scale show to $2,400 or more for a regional or national show. Take a tough look at the purposes of a trade show and determine if a trade show really does allow your company to find clients and/or buyers of its products and services. If it only provides an opportunity to see people and be seen by them, that probably isn't enough.

Setting objectives

Setting very specific objectives for your trade show participation allows you to accurately direct every effort you make for the show, from training personnel who will staff the booth to drafting written materials and determining which potential clients to take out to lunch or dinner.

For example, if your product or service is aimed at the general public, your objective may be to "take orders for X widgets" or to "generate X solid leads for follow-up sales approaches." In these cases, because you are looking for high quantity, you need to capture your audience with much more than an approach that merely says, "Look at our booth so you'll remember us later."

Consider the approach used by many marine insurance agencies when they exhibit at boat shows. They know most people come to see the boats, and they also know that an insurance agency doesn't have a product to "show." So, they try to make sure their booth is well placed in a central location and marked by balloons, banners, and possibly even some interesting boating films or videos. They staff it with plenty of trained personnel who are ready to smile and offer, "I'd like to tell you about our outstanding insurance service record," to people who just slow down as they are walking by. But most important, they are ready to *sign up clients on the spot*.

They have stacks of forms to be completed by a boat owner about his/her boat. Then, on the spot, they use that information to calculate the cost of insurance and to determine if someone qualifies for it. If the visitor does, he/she receives a binder number immediately, with a policy and invoice to follow. This is a much more active and successful approach than "here's my card and brochure; give me a call." The more you can do to get a client or customer "hooked" while still at the show, the more likely you are to meet your objectives.

Reaching distributors

Because trade shows have grown so rapidly in number, and because you want to get the most for the money it costs to participate, one of the most important questions you'll need to answer is: Which show(s) do I want to attend? What shows do my targets attend? Then, think of the possibility of reaching those people in a less direct manner such as through agents and distributors (middlemen) who in turn reach your client or customer.

It may make much more sense to participate in a trade show attended by agents or distributors than one attended by end users. For example, Laura McVain started a business that represents several ski resorts in their nationwide marketing. She participates in trade shows as their representative, but she doesn't look for shows that would be attended by skiers who might visit the resorts. Instead, she goes to shows that are attended by travel agents who guide skiers to the resorts she represents. At the trade shows, she runs videos of the resorts, provides brochures about the areas and their amenities, and entertains travel agents in a hospitality suite after trade show hours.

Prospecting opportunities

To come away from the show with a list of blue-chip prospects for follow-up, such as agents who might not actually buy or sign up for anything on the spot but who are worth your time in terms of follow-up contacts, start by asking the association sponsoring the show for a list of attendees. From that list, begin selecting your potential prospects and send them, ahead of time, some information about your company and an invitation to visit your trade show exhibit.

Follow this up with phone calls and try to arrange specific times to meet with some of the individuals you have targeted during the week of the show. The group you have targeted for their high potential will, during the show, slowly narrow down to a smaller group of actual prospects—people you'll keep in touch with after the trade show.

Follow-up

What will you do to follow-up on the contacts you've made during the trade show? Interest can evaporate quickly if it isn't nurtured. You'll need to stay in touch with contacts you made at the trade show to continue to provide them with information about your products or services. And this is a good way to demonstrate the personal contact you can provide. By doing a good job of follow-up, you maximize your trade show investment.

Planning

If you have not exhibited before, you'll have plenty of homework to do before attempting such a venture. It's easy enough to make a horrible showing the first time out if you have no idea of the level of preparation and professionalism required to be successful.

The best people to send to the trade show are trained personnel who are informed and enthusiastic about your service or product. This could be you or others on your staff. However, have you noticed how many exhibits are hosted by local temporary personnel whose only prior information is the location of the booth they are handling?

It is very tempting to hire "on location," because these people don't need to fly from somewhere to attend or to be put up in a hotel. If you do hire local assistance, however, you'll need to give them plenty of back-up support in terms of knowledgable individuals from the main office and training prior to the show. Otherwise, don't do it.

The companies that are most thorough in this regard assemble everybody involved in their exhibit, including company employees, the day before the opening. At that time, they clarify objectives, train local temporary personnel, and prepare a schedule for "working" the booth. Everyone gets the same message about how to handle interested show attendees and how to best represent the company.

One trade show marketing planner suggests informing people who work on the show about the costs involved. When your staff knows the cost of exhibiting, and how important it might be to the company, they will act accordingly.

Exhibiting is not for everyone, however. On the down side, you and/or members of your staff will be engaged for two or three days at the show, and counting preparation and post-show activities, you can easily tie up a minimum of 10- to 12-person days. On top of the cost of the show, other related expenses, and the work pile up back at the office, why do trade shows continue to be so popular among small business entrepreneurs?

Jeff Stevens, a marketing representative for Phoenix Radiology in Chatsworth, California, comments, "Where else are you going to meet so many potential targets in such a short time? And why worry about the problems back at the office. There will always be problems, and when you get back, you'll take care of them just like you always do."

Convinced that trade shows might be for you? If so, a good first step would be to attend one, with a new perspective. Critically examine which booths attract your eye and why. Stevens advises, "note the type of signs and displays being used, hand-outs and other promotional materials, and the dress, demeanor, and accessibility of those working the booth." Also, ask exhibitors about their experiences and the benefits they've derived.

Get the name of the show's management group and ask for a copy of their exhibitor instructions and guidelines. Most shows have them and they represent a valuable free source of information. Finally, call several local graphic art services and audio-visual suppliers to determine what it would cost to develop the type of exhibit you want to present.

Joe Jeff Goldblatt, former President of the Wonder Company, a Nashville, Tennessee-based special events production company, suggests the following 16 tips to boost booth sales:

1. Send potential attendees (prospects) a printed piece containing an offer.

2. Make the offer strong enough to motivate them to come buy! Strong offers include free items, major discounts good only on the day of the show, and free information and consulting.

3. Design the booth to allow optimum room to demonstrate the product and to negotiate the sale.

4. Make certain the product is illuminated well and is the central focus of the booth design.

5. Ask for business cards for a drawing that will be held after the show.

6. Display the "prize" next to the entry vessel so the prospect can easily see what he might win.

7. Prepare a short, five-question survey that includes space to write down the client's first name and company name;

prior knowledge or use of your product; annual needs for your services; current satisfaction with the product they are now using; and their ability to make a decision to try your product.

8. When appropriate, ask the salespeople to try to close sales in the booth. Use the advertised offer as the entry to closing. "Did you receive our special offer in the mail?"

9. Always keep the conversation focused on the product.

10. Be concise, direct, and engaging. The average booth visit is less than one minute! You are producing a live commercial.

11. Keep something sweet, such as candy or other items, in the booth to sweeten up your clients! (If acceptable to trade show management.)

12. Visit all other booths 15 minutes to opening and tell salespeople of your location and special offer.

13. Consider using a free, instant photo give-away with an imprinted photo mount for your clients.

14. Make certain that each prospect leaves as a potential client. Give them printed material with your name and phone number so they can follow-up.

15. Rest the day before the trade show. Treat the trade show as a chance to appear in the olympics of your industry. Train!

16. Training includes rehearsing and role playing with your salespeople. Rehearse a script so that it becomes a natural and honest conversation with the potential client.

Finally, remember: the *prize* always equals the *price*. If you want a high return, then out plan and out perform everyone else and you will win every time!

Visiting trade shows

Visiting, rather than exhibiting in a trade show, is, of course, less costly. Plan your time at the show carefully, visiting the firms you would like as customers. Maximize your time by visiting the press or information area and obtaining a list of exhibitors and their locations. Talk with the exhibitors who could be likely customers for you, but don't come on too strong. After all, they're the ones exhibiting, not you. Simply leave your business card.

If there is time, and the corporate representatives are too busy, obtain the names, addresses, and phone numbers for the small business vendor coordinator or appropriate purchasing agent. Try to procure copies of supplier lists for use in identifying potential customers for your firm. You might not be able to get all of this information as a visitor, but the contact you've made is still valuable.

Once you are back in your office, be sure to follow up on whatever contacts or information you've developed. The contacts you've met also met 200 other people at the show, so your follow-up must be swift, informative and professional. The following is a quick summary of the benefits you can derive through trade shows:

- Demonstrate new products
- Find new customers
- Take orders
- Develop mailing lists
- Promote the company image
- Determine what competitors are doing

If you haven't considered them before, don't overlook the significant marketing opportunities trade shows can offer. It's an investment that can pay off in a big way. Corporate America meets at trade shows, and you should be there, too. Appendix C contains a listing of association and convention sources that you might find helpful.

10

Determining customer needs

PURCHASING AGENTS CONSIDER A VARIETY OF FACTORS WHEN MAKING purchase decisions. To compete successfully for business, find out what the customer's needs are.

Categorizing customer needs

Critical needs can be categorized into the three groups: quality standards, service, and price.

1. Standards of quality:

   - Can you meet them with current equipment/personnel?
   - If your product greatly exceeds the standards, will your price be too high?
   - Is your level of quality consistent over time?

2. Service required:

   - Do you currently provide the appropriate services for your customer?
   - Is your normal level of service sufficient or will you need to allocate additional resources to provide the expected services to this customer?

3. Price

- Does this customer consider only price when making a purchasing decision?
- Can you offer something more than your competitors for the same price?
- Are the "extras" you offer—higher quality, better service—worth the increased price you charge?

You must always be digging to find out what buyers expect from suppliers in the service levels, lead times, and delivery schedules, etc. Also, you need to know what help or exceptions they might be willing to give you in terms of technical assistance, financial assistance, and timing of payments.

After you have acquired a customer, communication becomes even more important. Keep in touch with the customer on a regular basis to give him/her progress reports and be available when the customer wants to meet with you. If at all possible, return customers' calls promptly. If you cannot, have your assistant call and explain that you are tied up with meetings, etc., and that you will call as soon as you are free.

Implementing a cost reduction program

The hallmark of an effective cost reduction program is characterized by the supplier who *always* strives to reduce costs without reducing quality as opposed to ineffective displays of obsequious efforts. Seek out the advice of your employees for new methods of production, improved materials handling, streamlining work flow, and new sources of suppliers. Across the board, purchasing agents agree that they expect suppliers to continuously be seeking new ways to effectively reduce costs.

Can the job be done with fewer parts? Will your product require less frequent maintenance? Will it be easier to store and transport? Let customers know that you're working to help them. At Digital Equipment Company purchasing agents are on constant alert to identify and retain such vendors. Customers appreciate your passing on any reduced costs and tend to want to keep working with you—who wouldn't?

Meeting conformance standards

You should know what your customers' standards are. It is better to know in advance and determine if you can meet them than to have your product rejected as unacceptable. This prior knowledge will save you money—what you don't have to spend on reworking items or purchasing new equipment. More important, knowledge of conformance standards and your ability to meet them will establish and enhance your firm's reputation.

Innovation

A good way to indicate your propensity towards innovation is to ask your customers if there is a product or service they need or want. Many profitable, innovative relationships between buyers and suppliers started because the supplier asked such a question. Indeed, many corporations such as Stanadyne and Boise Cascade have initiated progressive programs that actively encourage supplier-initiated innovation.

Is there a better way to service your customer? Can you find new uses for an old product? Do you see any potential for developing a new or improved distribution method? Are there new production methods that could lower costs while maintaining quality? Find out and tell them of the improvements. The following tips can help you to maintain a reputation for innovation and customer service:

- Never be "out of stock."
- Keep a small supply of extra parts on hand for items you currently handle.
- Provide suggestions to the buyer on maintaining your product.

Emergency contingency planning

If a customer had a fire or flood, could your firm be flexible enough to meet his/her emergency needs? Could you provide additional inventory to him/her? Provide space for storage? Provide a rush order or provide special distribution for the customer?

By discussing these needs in advance with the customer, you will demonstrate your concern and provide the "something extra" that will make your firm stand out.

Implementing a quality control program

Certain types of products require uncommonly close adherence to specifications, which are normally clearly defined in the contract.

A description of your quality control program tells the buyers that you have a formal, documented system for evaluating your product according to predetermined standards.

A quality control program can be a point in your favor when your firm is producing on a contract that requires adherence to specifications. The customer might want to inspect the product at your plant before it is shipped or at his plant after it is received.

Quality control is also important for service firms. If you have this program, tell the customer. If you don't have such a program, consider developing one if it suits your type of service.

Developing a quality control program for manufacturers

As a manufacturer or distributor, you most likely have established a procedure to ensure quality products or services. It's one thing to tell a purchasing agent that you have a system for quality control, but unless your assurance is backed up with a written plan or manual, you might not be considered for a contract. A quality assurance program indicates to purchasing agents that you consider quality to be a vital factor and that you have taken the time to think through and prepare a real quality control system.

In the troubled economy of the early 1980s, price might have overridden quality as a deciding factor in selecting suppliers. Increasingly, however, purchasing managers are acknowledging that higher quality ultimately means lower costs for their corporations. Additionally, increasing foreign imports dictate a higher domestic quality level than ever before.

A prime responsibility of purchasing managers is to analyze all supplier qualifications and standards in detail. The purchasing manager's review of your written plan for quality assurance is the first step in documenting quality control, often followed by an on-site visit to your plant or distribution warehouse to observe your quality assurance plan in action.

The typical purchasing executive will make from five to ten trips a year to check out existing or potential suppliers, and they spend a great deal of time selecting the right suppliers for their raw materials and big-ticket items. Figure 10-1 shows a sample vendor visitation report form. The items contained on the form are typical of the type of information a purchasing department is likely to seek when visiting your shop.

In chapter 5, we looked at what information you needed to document your capabilities before your presentation to a corporate

VENDOR VISITATION REPORT

1. Company name _____

   Address _____

   Town _____ State _____ Zip _____

   Telephone _____

2. Purpose of trip _____
3. Principals, titles, and evaluation

   a. Manufacturing _____
   b. Marketing _____
   c. Administration _____
   d. Financial _____
   e. Logistics _____

4. Representatives

   a. _____
   b. _____
   c. _____

5. Volume of business _____
6. Principal products or services _____
7. Union and contract dates _____
8. Vendor key suppliers _____
9. Facilities (brief description) _____

   a. Building and size _____
   b. Shipping and receiving facilities _____
   c. Housekeeping: Poor _____ Good _____ Excellent _____

10. Equipment

    a. Type and condition _____
    b. Capable of future expansion: Yes _____ No _____

11. Quality assurance program: Yes _____ No _____

    Comments _____
12. Approved vendor for _____
13. Comments _____

Fig. 10-1. A vendor visitation report.

buyer. If, and when, the buyer visits you on site, you must present even greater detail about your operations.

Vendor visitation reports

Many large corporations send representatives to visit small vendor plants. The vendor visitation report shown in Fig. 10-1 includes just some of the items corporate giants will want to review. General

Motors, Ingersoll-Rand, and Seagram all make visits to small vendor plants. Here's what you can expect:

- The inspection will most likely be conducted by a team that could include the purchasing agent, an engineer, and the corporation's own quality control person.
- The inspection team will probably look for quality control based on statistical process control techniques, not just finished goods inspection.
- The inspectors will want a demonstration of the policies that are implemented at the operating level, not just at final inspection. They will look for process controls, including proper training for workers, that reduce the likelihood of error.
- They might want to review scrap and rework records. Low scrap and rework levels indicates that productivity is up.

The following is a list of the components of a complete quality assurance plan for manufacturers and distributors. Corporate visitors are apt to want to know about how you handle:

- Organization (chart)
- Staff responsibilities
- Documentation, records, and corrective action
- Measuring and test equipment
- Process control
- Indication of inspection status
- Customer-furnished materials
- Nonconforming materials
- Sampling inspections
- Alternative inspection provisions
- Receiving inspection
- Customer evaluation
- Segregation control
- Drawing and change control
- Purchasing and certification
- Support documents

Organization chart   An organization chart shows the lines of command and responsibility in your company and illustrates the interrelated functions of different departments or personnel.

Responsibilities   Responsibilities specify that all employees of the company are responsible for adherence to quality requirements and must be active participants in all quality control programs. Also, specifies the chain of command from the president through the quality manager and quality-control inspectors.

Documentation, records, and corrective action   Documentation, records, and corrective action requires a specific quality-control plan for each job. The size and complexity of the job will determine the detail needed. The completion of the plan requires development of detailed inspection sheets for each part, assembly, and unit. Because the inspection sheets are operating procedures for the quality inspectors, they must be clear, complete, and current.

Each form should include basic contract identification data, specific drawing and drawing revision data, the name of the inspector, and the type of inspection. The body of the inspection sheet explains what procedure is to be done, any special testing or measuring restrictions, and approval/rejection criteria. The form should also specify the test equipment necessary to perform required inspections.

If an item is rejected, a note is placed on the inspection sheet and a nonconformance report is completed that details the number and type of deficiencies found, their causes, and the steps taken to correct them. It also describes action taken to prevent recurrence of the problem.

Measuring and test equipment   Measuring and test equipment discusses intervals for calibration checks; measurement standards traceable to the National Bureau of Standards; necessity of periodic review of the adequacy of standards; control over environmental conditions; calibration procedures; calibration sources; records showing calibration intervals, certification date, and results of the last calibration; calibration labeling; and government verification.

This section should also include procedures for test equipment found to be out of tolerance—nothing works perfectly indefinitely. It's a solid demonstration of integrity to identify what's out of tolerance and why, and how and when the equipment was/will be properly adjusted.

Process control   Process control includes parts of the certain processes, such a plating, radiography, or heat treating that do not lend themselves to after-the-fact inspection. Thus, quality assurance inspections are necessary while the work is being performed. This section outlines procedures for work-in-process controls.

Indication of inspection status   Quality assurance inspections are performed during four phases—at receiving, in process, first article, and final—on all material and supplies used on all jobs having a quality-control requirement. An item is either accepted or rejected at each of these points.

"Accept" tags should provide the following information: item, job number, drawing number, lot number, type of inspection, quantity accepted for each inspection, date of inspection, and quality-control inspector's initial or stamp.

"Reject" tags indicate the cause of rejection, in addition to all information on the "accept" tag. A "hold" category describes pieces that have not been accepted or rejected. The tag indicates why a given item or lot is not tagged as an accept or reject.

Customer-furnished material   Customer furnished materials describes procedures used to inspect, identify, and protect materials furnished by the customer. The "accept" or "reject" tags described above are used to identify the status of the inspected materials.

Nonconforming material   Nonconforming materials describe the procedures for identification, segregation, presentation, and disposition of rework or repaired supplies. The nonconforming item will remain in nonconforming storage until a decision is made, in consultation with the customer, to offer as is, to rework, to repair, or to scrap the item.

Sampling inspections   Sampling inspections establishes sampling inspection procedures for use when large quantities of like items are manufactured and the customer approves a sampling inspection.

Alternative inspection provisions   Alternative inspection provisions specify that the provisions customer and an authorized vendor representative must approve all changes to inspection procedures and inspection equipment other than that specified in the initial contract.

Receiving inspection   Receiving inspection describes the procedure for quality inspection of all material and supplies received by the company.

Customer evaluation   Customer evaluation establishes procedures for review by all customers who request an evaluation of the company's quality assurance program. Specifies that requests will be honored.

Segregation control   Segregation control ensures that all materials requiring quality certification will be inspected, tagged, and placed in a segregated storage area.

Drawing and change control   Drawing and change control specifies procedures to ensure that any old drawings are properly destroyed and that new drawings and changes are correctly logged and attached to drawings for the appropriate foreman or department head.

Purchasing and certification   Purchasing and certification specifies the procedure for quality assurance of purchasing of materials and services by you.

Supporting documents   Supporting documents can include:

- Traveler/reject tag
- Receiving inspection report
- Nonconformance report
- Nonconformance report supplement
- Detailed inspection procedure and record
- Instrument calibration forms
- Certificate of compliance
- Stores inventory log
- Drawing revision/change record
- Drawing control log
- Operating procedures for precision measuring equipment
- Checklist for evaluation of contractor's calibration system

An aspect of quality assurance that might be overlooked is the appearance of your plant or warehouse and delivery vehicles. A product that has passed stringent quality-control measurements but is delivered to the customer in a dirty truck makes a very poor first impression. Don't attempt a two-minute drill to improve plant and equipment appearance right before you're about to be visited. Maintain them all the time. A well-kept appearance of your facility and equipment will indicate to customers that your quality assurance plan permeates every aspect of your company.

A typical Quality Assurance Procedures Manual can range from 25 to 85 pages. The types of products you produce and your size, however, might necessitate a manual that is longer or shorter.

It's vital to have a realistic, specific, quality-control plan and to implement it consistently. Quality control is the name of the game, and your plan will demonstrate that you play by the rules.

Developing a quality control program for service firms

Quality control has always been considered the arena of manufacturing—measuring the quality of manufactured products against definable standards. Companies that provide services to a client, however, have more at stake in developing a quality assurance program than manufacturing companies simply because their outcome and products are more difficult to measure. Most important, the quality of your service is the basic factor separating you from the ever-burgeoning number of your competitors.

Developing a comprehensive quality assurance program for your service company, indicates to a potential client that you care about the quality of your service, and that you realize the importance of controlling it from start to finish.

Components of an effective service industry quality assurance program include:

- Appointing a quality assurance director or team.
- Monitoring time in an organized manner.
- Developing a procedure for checking services in process.
- Developing forms for internal communication and forms for communication with the client.
- Building flexibility into your program to meet the requirement of specific projects.

Appointing a quality assurance director

Depending on the size of your company and the number of projects you handle at one time, you should appoint or assign a quality assurance director and involve others as part of a quality assurance project team. This task is often the responsibility of the project director and in good firms is *always* taken care of. The major job responsibility of the quality assurance director is to coordinate the overall schedule of work, oversee all client communication, and be responsible for the quality and timeliness of all deliverables.

It is a good idea to include a checklist of the quality assurance director's specific responsibilities in your company's brochure.

Once a contract has been received, outline the educational qualifications of all the people who will work on that particular project, as well as their responsibilities for specific aspects of the project.

Developing a "work in process" check

A procedure should be developed to check the work of personnel involved in each project, not only as each deliverable is finished, but also while work is in progress. In an architectural firm, for example, the quality assurance director should review the specs and plans, develop a checklist for items to be included in each working drawing, handle communication with others affected by the building (such as the fire marshall), and ensure project feasibility for its duration.

Monitoring time

Accounting for billed time must involve a well-developed system that allows you to monitor all personnel and their daily progress on tasks and subtasks. Several computer software programs are available for time management, but typed or handwritten forms are just as useful. Summary sheets describing time billed to each task or subtask of the project should be made available to the quality assurance director each week. This will indicate that the project is on track and enable you to spot any problems quickly. Also, the quality assurance director will be able to notify the customer well in advance of the deadline if a delivery date must be delayed.

Developing communication forms

Forms allow concise communication. Properly distributing internal forms will ensure that everyone on the project is aware of any changes in the scope of the work. You will also want to develop external forms. Some service companies develop intricate forms in order to impress clients, but a complicated form might merely confuse a client. Use forms that communicate both the message and intent easily.

Building flexibility into your program

Although your core program of quality assurance will remain the same, each project has its differences. Depending on the size and complexity of the job, you might opt to use a quality assurance director or a team to handle quality control. A quality assurance program should be developed for each project, inserting the deliverables schedule, schedule of reporting, and only forms that will be used according to the needs of the specific job.

Because a service can be difficult to measure, it is all the more important that you plan and outline your efforts. You will have more flexibility than a manufacturer in both designing your plan and implementing it, and your propensity toward innovation in quality control will stand you in good stead with potential and existing customers. The key question to ask your clients is: "How will you and I know when the job has been done correctly?"

Below is a summary of the minimum information requirements for marketing to major corporations when calling on them or if they are visiting you. It is synthesis of the suggestions in chapter 6 and the material in this chapter.

Whether your company is a manufacturer, a service company, or something in between, quality control and assurance program will help keep large buyers happy.

The following is a quick summary of the minimum of information arsenal you'll need to woo major corporations:

1. **Capability profile/statement/business plan**

    A. Ownership—Sole proprietors, partnerships, or corporations should list major stockholders. Include an organization chart.

    B. Products/Services—Describe your firm's product or service clearly and completely and the market you serve.

    C. Location(s)—List the addresses and telephone numbers of your locations.

    D. Projects/Activities—Concisely describe recent jobs your firm had undertaken on which you performed well.

    E. References/Testimonials—If you have received favorable letters commending your firm and the jobs you have done, include copies (first, get permission from the author of the letter). If you have satisfied customers, ask them if you could use their names as references for potential customers.

    F. Description of Your Firm—List the key members of your firm, their specialties, their experience, and how long your firm has been in business.

    G. Goals—Describe what your goals are for specific customers, what product or service you want to provide, and what level of service you will provide.

2. **Technical capability**

   A. Human—Describe the number of skilled employees you have and their specialties and experience and the number of unskilled employees.

   B. Equipment—List the number of, and types, of machinery, include capacity and age.

3. **Quality**

   A. Conformance Standards—If the customer has specifications you must meet, explain your checks to determine adherence to the specifications.

   B. Guarantees/Warranties—Describe any guarantee for your product/service. If you do warrant your product, outline its scope.

   C. Quality Assurance Program—If your firm has an established program to monitor quality of production, briefly describe it and its benefits.

   D. Measurement Capability (Testing and Inspection)—Any equipment used for testing and inspecting should be itemized. Explain the tolerance-range capacity of the equipment.

4. **Facility and financial capability**

   A. Manufacturing/Assembly Size and Capacity—State the size of your plant (square foot), and the daily output of your plant at maximum operating level.

   B. Equipment List—Type, capacity, and quality.

   C. Financial Position—Provide your balance sheet, your profit and loss statement, and information on line of credit—if you have one.

5. **Price**

   A. Additional Charges—Identify and Itemize any charge for set up, initial charges, development, engineering, tooling, special equipment, testing, materials, and machinery.

   B. Competitiveness—Provide your best price, best quality, and best delivery date.

   C. Meeting Customer Needs—List your understanding of the customer's requirements and how you plan to meet them.

D. Other Considerations—How do you handle overruns or damaged goods?

6. **Labor**

   A. Availability of Workers—Skilled workers, semi-skilled workers, and unskilled workers.

   B. Hourly Rates—List the hourly rates for your current employee(s), and any required additions to your work force for this job.

   C. Union/Nonunion—Clarify whether you are union or nonunion. Do you reside in a right-to-work state?

7. **Security**

   A. Confidentiality—Guarantee that customer's trade secrets, confidential information, and new product plans will not be divulged. Describe how you will accomplish this.

   B. Plant Security—Describe your security measures for your plant, office, storage yard, and documents.

Most vendors do not want to take the time and effort to determine customers' needs or implement a comprehensive quality control program. Those who do fare far better in terms of doing volume business with corporate giants.

11

Becoming a successful bidder and negotiator

WHEN YOU SUBMIT A BID TO A PURCHASER AND COMPETE WITH OTHER vendors seeking the same contract, your bid must be superior. You must go beyond the standard requirements and offer the extra edge that will set you apart. Generally, the extra edge is not price related.

Promise the highest quality product that *you can deliver* using current employees and equipment. If the buyer has specification requirements, make sure you can equal or exceed them. Then accurately assess your scheduling and delivery abilities. Don't promise what you can't deliver in an attempt to secure the contract. This is the quickest route to failure.

Determining your break-even point

To estimate a fair and competitive price that will yield a profit, you'll want to perform a break-even analysis. To determine production costs, first distinguish your fixed costs from your variable costs. Fixed costs generally do not vary with changes in the number of units produced or sold. The cost of renting your premises, for example, does not change because your production doubles. Rent might increase over time, but not because you're producing more.

Total variable costs change directly with changes in the number of units you produce or sell. Variable costs per unit are constant, that is, twice as many workers and twice as much material produce twice as much product X. Your total cost is the sum of all your fixed costs and your total variable costs.

Your total revenue figure is derived by multiplying price times quantity. If you sell 10,000 units of X at $10, total revenue is $100,000. Profits are whatever is left of the $100,000 after all expenses are paid.

Figure 11-1 illustrates the relationship between costs, revenue, profits, and losses in determining the break-even point. Knowing the number of units you need to sell to break even is important in setting the price. If you find that a product priced at $100 per unit has a variable cost of $60 per unit, then the contribution per unit to fixed costs is $40. With total fixed costs of $120,000, your break-even point in *units* is determined as follows:

$$\text{Break-even point} = \frac{\text{fixed costs}}{\text{per unit contribution to fixed costs}}$$

$$\text{Break-even point} = \frac{\$120,000}{\$40/\text{unit}}$$

$$= 3,000 \text{ units}$$

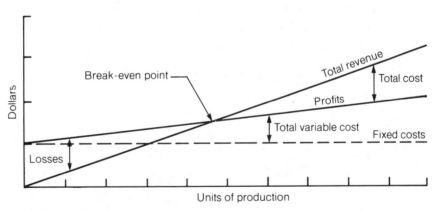

Fig. 11-1. The break-even point.

So, with a $40 per unit contribution to fixed costs (hence a $40 gross profit margin per unit), you must sell 3,000 units to break even. Above the break-even point of 3,000 units, in this example, the per unit contribution to fixed costs goes to profits. For example, if you sell 3,001 units, profit equals $40. Each additional unit that sell, above 3,000 units, adds another $40 to your profits.

To calculate your break-even point in terms of dollar sales volume, multiply your break-even point in units by the price per unit. In the previous example, the break-even point in terms of dollar sales volume would be 3,000 (units) times $100, which equals $300,000.

$$3000 \text{ units} \times \$1000 \text{ price/unit} = \$300,000$$

Service provisions and other safeguards

Your bid price should also take into consideration the cost of providing service. If you can guarantee your service in your bid, that's a big plus.

In recent years, product liability has become a major legal issue. Manufacturers of component parts, as well as end manufacturers, are often sued. So, state right in your bid whether or not you will assume responsibility for product liability. If you do, be sure that your insurance covers it.

Avoiding the mid-project slump You score points if, somewhere in your bid, you assure the customer that your firm maintains a continuous or increasing level of performance.

When a company begins to achieve at least a moderate level of success, it often makes the mistake of letting its "guard" down. You work hard to win new customers, and you work hard to maintain them. Avoiding the mid-project slump is a taxing but rewarding experience, because this often means you've successfully avoided the project deadline crunch. See Fig. 11-2.

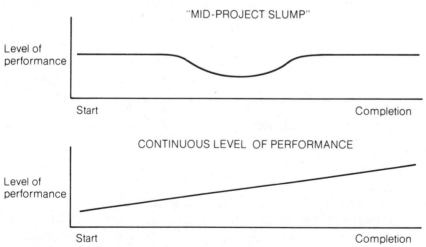

Fig. 11-2. A typical project activity chart.

Shortchanging your need for legal assistance   All of the giants to whom you'd like to sell to employ full-time legal specialists, and many maintain elaborately layered legal departments. There will be times when you should use an attorney skilled in general contract and business law, more so with increasing revenues. Contacting an attorney *before* a contract or bid is signed can prevent problems.

Understanding contract law

Existing government regulation of monopolistic and unfair trade practices directly affects, and benefits, small businesses. While the various acts summarized in this section might not become household words to you, they do merit brief mention.

The U.S. Department of Justice enforces the Sherman Antitrust Act, which outlaws monopolies and all types of business combinations formed to restrain trade or commerce. The Clayton Act was designed to prohibit practices that might substantially lessen competition or tend to create a monopoly. The Robinson-Patman Act is actually an amendment to the Clayton Act and gives the Federal Trade Commission authority to eliminate quantity discounts and prohibit promotional allowances except on an equal bases. All three of these acts are enforced by the U.S. Department of Justice.

The Federal Trade Commission, a separate and distinct U.S. government federal agency, prohibits unfair methods of competition and unfair and deceptive acts and practices in commerce. Many corporations, such as Hewlitt Packard and 3M, state their compliance procedures in their supplier guides.

The Federal Trade Commission has identified certain types of activities as unfair business practices. These include:

- Making false and inaccurate statements about competitors' products and/or their businesses.
- Selling rebuilt, secondhand, or old articles as new.
- Simulating trade names or labels of competitors and affixing them to your own product.
- Bribing customers or employees to obtain patronage.
- Buying up supplies to hamper competitors.
- Stifling or eliminating competition.

While the previous items are labeled as unfair, the Federal Trade Commission considers the following items to be unlawful:

- Price fixing
- Exclusive deals
- False and deceptive advertising
- Price discrimination
- Payment of brokerage to buyers

All contracts are negotiable

Between the time when you make a bid (or request to bid) on a contract let by a major corporation and the time you actually win the contract award, a substantial amount of negotiating might occur. All contracts are based on face-to-face exchanges between buyers and sellers. The terms and methods by which the contract will be fulfilled is a prerequisite to a mutually favorable business transaction.

The initial step in becoming a skilled negotiator, then, is to do your homework. Dr. Chester A. Karrass, Gerald I. Nierenberg, and other top negotiators agree that the best negotiators are well pre-pared and have done lots of homework before ever entering into the negotiation process.

First, establish your objectives. Why are you seeking a particu-lar contract? The answer might be obvious but ask yourself this question nevertheless. Will your bid price produce a profit for your company? Are you seeking a long-term relationship? How will you meet or exceed contract requirements? These are the types of questions you are likely to be asked at any point in the process of calling on, and triumphantly marketing to, the corporate giants.

The next component of negotiation preparation is to examine your capabilities. For example, what advantages do you have over your competitors, particularly in the areas of technology, produc-tion, manufacturing, scheduling, or other performance factors? What are your financial needs to complete this contract? Will you seek assistance from the buyer or can you carry all of the costs internally? What are your cash flow requirements for the duration of the contract?

Tactical decisions

Effective negotiators must make tactical decisions before entering into the negotiation process. Will you negotiate as an individual or will you use a team? This will depend largely on the importance of the negotiation, the time available, and the skills required to successfully close the deal. When selecting a negotiating team, be certain that each member has a specific function. Each person should know the agreed upon strategy and objectives, have a specialty, and demonstrate his or her confidence. Everyone is there to be a productive member of the negotiating team, therefore, clear up any internal disagreements you might have well in advance of the negotiation. The advantages to using a single negotiator include the following:

- It prevents a "divide and conquer" strategy by opponents.
- It demonstrates that you have complete responsibility.
- It eliminates a weakened position resulting from differences of opinion among team members.
- It facilitates on-the-spot decision-making, particularly in the area of granting or receiving concessions.
- It fosters a one-on-one relationship with the buyer.

Another component of effective negotiation is to determine in advance what you really want to get from the negotiation and for what terms you will settle. Purchasing agents are most receptive now than ever before to your ideas on improving their operations. Your good ideas are negotiating tools.

In many ways, negotiation is like a poker game in that you don't really reveal the cards until after you have won. When you first start negotiating, it is not wise to reveal the exact terms that you want. Usually, at the beginning of a negotiation, both the buyer and the seller will state what they are seeking, and usually, these positions seem unreasonable to one another. Throughout the course of the negotiation, each side will make counter proposals and concessions until, hopefully, mutually agreeable positions are reached. Ask for more, recognizing that the resulting compromises will eventually come closer to your initial, unrevealed position.

Listen and rebut

Corporate purchasing agents negotiate far more often than you with greater results. If they're part of a top purchasing department such as Union Carbide, General Foods, or Monsanto, then they've received top training. Also, purchasing agents are privy to the excellent array of audio-visual training materials available through their industry associations. "Do not go gentle into that good night." You need to bone up on negotiating.

Negotiation trainer Neil Rackham observes that the best negotiators carefully listen to the points presented by the other side. Then they attack those points, indicating that they listened and they understood what the other side said, that they agree in part with some of the points made, but they disagree with "X,Y,Z" and "here is why." This is far superior, believes Rackham, then politely listening to the other party and then launching full scale into what you want to say without addressing and staying on top of what your opponent has just said.

The best negotiators choose their words and tone of voice carefully. Try to pose questions in a way that does not offend or threaten. Good negotiators have notes prepared and take notes during the negotiations. One of the best tactics for assuring a successful negotiation is to find out, in advance, the time constraints or deadline that your opponent faces. People are more agreeable when facing a deadline. Don't let your opponent know that you know his deadline, however.

One key negotiating tactic many purchasing agents have been taught to display is what Dr. Karrass calls the "double finch." Whenever you or your marketing representatives quote a price, the purchasing agent is taught to say "Holy Cow," or its equivalent. If this corporate purchasing division has really followed their training, both the agent and his boss will say it distinctly and within your earshot.

Another strategy mastered by purchasing agents is to avoid addressing the issue of price, particularly after you have made a quote. This tends to raise your anxieties, slowly putting pressure on you. The purchasing agent knows darn well what price you quoted and that you are interested in getting some kind of confirmation. His measured reluctance in giving you that confirmation is all part of a master plan.

If you're not aware of these types of tactics, you are likely to buckle on your price or on some other major provision, perhaps only moments before you were about to get what you asked for.

Your bottom line

Your bid should reflect complete cost information. Before entering the negotiation, you will have determined your "bottom line bid," under which you cannot go because to do so would cause your firm to lose money on the contract. Therefore, rather than cut or lower the price when faced with a difficult negotiation, instead, modify service and/or delivery terms that you can readily offer cost effectively.

Be ready to present a counter proposal. Most entrepreneurs overlook, or worse, don't have, the foresight to do this. During negotiations, it might be difficult to accurately assess the impact of suggested positions. Anticipate these before negotiating so you know what the net effect of an alternative will be. Perhaps dividing a job into three separate tasks to run consecutively will better serve the client and be more manageable for you.

In advance of the negotiation proceedings, you might determine what the effects would be of dividing one big job into three from management, production, and administrative and cost standpoints. The supplier who comes to the negotiating table with effective counter proposals has a feather in his cap.

Standing out from the crowd

A purchasing coordinator for a midwestern company indicated several areas in which suppliers needed to improve in dealing with corporate purchasing departments, including understanding the corporate procurement cycle, maintaining non-adverse relationships when faced with delays, financing large jobs, and computing job costs, particularly overhead costs.

Some suppliers who are confronted with their first opportunity to do business with a large corporation make the mistake of underbidding, either because they have not properly computed internal costs or in hopes of winning the contract to get a foot in the door. Either reason is dangerous and could lead to disastrous results, including a lower-quality product than agreed upon, slower delivery, and finally customer dissatisfaction.

Low bidding can wreak havoc on your cash flow, necessitate refinancing, and yield poor profits. The client will not be the only party dissatisfied. Low bidding tends to affect your own employees in terms of low morale, loss of confidence, and perhaps, burn out. If you're forced to make a low bid in order to win, abandon ship—there will be other voyages.

It is hard to tell you not to take some marginal jobs, especially when your plant or office is under-used, you have payroll to meet, or you "just know" that this contract will lead to great things. Yet, the battered dream of many suppliers is initiated in the form of low bidding.

Avoiding contract difficulties

The following are just some of the ways suppliers and contractors frequently run into trouble, followed by how one contractor, who we'll call SBC Limited's, avoids difficulties.

Failure to read with meticulous care the solicitation, its attachments, and specifications   SBC carefully reviews all materials contained in a request for proposal or solicitation. SBC also maintains familiarity with purchasing and procurement procedures, specifications, material allocation, delivery and supply expectations, and related matters. SBC obtains appropriate counsel when needed for advice on matters of bidder's rights and obligations, appeal procedures, termination, and default actions. Also, SBC is cognizant of the resources required for contract administration and the extensive documentation needed to successfully manage contracts.

Excessive optimism in assessing the task, the risk, and in-house capabilities   SBC takes a realistic approach in determining whether it has the overall capability, both technical and financial, to perform on selected projects. A delay in the receipt of goods and supplies from subcontractors, for example, could cause considerable setbacks during contract performance. These factors are taken into consideration when preparing bids, reviewing project plane, and awarding contracts. In addition, SBC approaches each solicitation critically and proceeds only after generating substantial evidence that the firm can successfully execute the contract.

Bidding on unreliable purchase descriptions or specifications   SBC immediately calls or writes for clarifications of unclear purchase or specification information whenever needed. SBC strives to ensure that any and all copies of the latest specifications revisions are obtained before submitting a bid.

Bidding based on estimates, not factual cost data   Many firms prepare cost estimate based on what they think will get the job. SBC prepares cost estimates on a per-bid basis, neither relying on previously prepared bids nor assuming that standard cost estimates or "ball park" figures will be sufficient. Key factors considered in any of SBC's bids include:

- Subcontractor and equipment vendor costs.
- Overhead and overhead rates.
- Learning curves for labor and salaried personnel.

- Estimate of person days required.
- Availability of government-furnished materials and equipment.
- Labor and salary rates and predictable changes.
- Profit potential.

Bidding under a time crunch   SBC maintains long-term monitoring and tracking on all significant business opportunities. SBC forgoes bidding on attractive solicitations when the deadline is not sufficient to prepare a thoroughly researched, double-checked bid.

Accepting an unrealistic time frame   SBC seeks only those projects wherein an acceptable time frame for project completion has been allotted. SBC finds it of no value to the firm, either in terms of cost, experience, or reputation, to bid on projects when it is known in advance that the time frame is unrealistic.

Accepting assignments beyond the state of the art Occasionally, corporations request creative and exploratory procurements that are negotiated with performance specifications. End products might include prototypes or test and evaluation models. While SBC is eager to conduct this type of project and has done so successfully in the past, SBC's highly capable, technically oriented staff carefully analyzes solicitations to determine if projects are, in fact, feasible.

Failure to take remedial action   SBC maintains a legal staff and appropriate resources to appeal claims made against the firm which SBC believes were done in error. This is an important strength for contractors.

Keeping your perspective

Even if you handle bidding and contracting as professionally as SBC, you might be prone to fall in love with what got you "there," made you successful, or seems to work okay. The following are three common pitfalls made by business owners and managers that can reduce the effectiveness of recent success:

1. *The idea that industry trends are predictable.* With the technological changes witnessed in recent years and the exponential technological advancement forthcoming, there will be few industries in which trends can be reasonably predicted beyond a few years. Technological changes are environmental factors that help foster dramatic shifts in

the economy, thereby upsetting or throwing off course what were thought to be industry trends might include:

- *Improved phone communications systems.* A greater reliance on conference calls and lesser frequency of small, on-site conferences.

- *Music synthesizers.* In a few years, 80 percent of all radio music will originate from a computer, not a musician. Studio musicians' jobs are now in jeopardy.

- *Developments in footwear.* The full line, "everything for everyone" shoe store is disappearing and is being replaced by athletic shoe stores, women's shoes only, men's shoes only, sandals and beach footwear, camping, hiking, and rough terrain shoe stores.

    For today's supplier, technological, environmental, or social factors can often undermine the objectives of the business and leave the manager wondering, "what went wrong?"

2. *Costs will change at a predictable rate.* In the past 10 years, we have seen the cost of energy and phone service more than triple. The minimum wage has risen several times and is due to go higher yet. Existing government regulations are now costing the average business manager as much as 15 percent of his time, while the dollars are as yet uncalculated.

    Inflation has cooled off, but it will be back, and maybe worse than before. The cost of water might rise dramatically. Other costs potentially rising above and beyond the predictable rate include office supplies, business insurance, and security and employee benefit packages. With both profit margins staying the same or declining slightly and operating costs inching ever upward, mammoth increases in the levels of business activity—volume—will be necessary to sustain viability.

3. *What worked before will work again.* This erroneous notion represents the greatest area of potential trouble for suppliers, because what worked before might not necessarily have anything to do with current or future business requirements. In professional services, success can often be a function of the uneven distribution of competitors within a geographic area. For smaller manufacturers, success is often based on the fact that product sales are not suf-

ficient for larger manufacturers to step in and overtake the particular market niche.

Unfortunately, past successes have only limited meaning for the future, and the best defense, as always, is to stay flexible and roll with the punches. Figure 11-3 is a good self-analysis checklist to use whenever you've been turned down for a job.

Why Didn't We Get The Job?

1. When you visited a potential buyer, were you or your salespeople:

   - Prepared? Knowledgeable of the customer's needs.
   - Knowledgeable of your product or service?
   - Dealing with the "right" person?
   - Capable of successfully completing the job you started?

2. Were you available when your customer tried to reach you:

   - Did you return his or her call promptly?
   - Did you keep the customer informed of progress *and* problems?
   - Did you deliver on time?
   - Were your reports comprehensive and well-prepared?

3. Consider the impression a visitor has of your office or plant:

   - Is it clean?
   - Are supplies stored conveniently yet out of the way?
   - Do your employees conduct themselves as "professionals?"
   - Would a fresh painting or cleaning improve it?

4. Remember that first impressions are lasting impressions. If too many defects caused a problem on previous contracts, examine all of the following areas to identify the problem, then correct it and prevent future problems:

   - Were defects caused by human or machine error?
   - How do you handle responsibility for defects? Don't assign blame. Give authority to deal with problem.
   - What is your frequency rate, the total number of defects compared to total number produced?
   - Does your quality-control program prevent defective items from leaving your shop? If not, what can you do to prevent this problem? Did you tell the customer your corrective actions?

Fig. 11-3. A self-analysis can help you pinpoint what went wrong.

Fig. 11-3. Continued.

5. With hidden and underlying problems, you must "look in the mirror" and be honest with yourself. Was the problem:

- Yourself. Trying to do too much yourself. Working 16 hour days, not delegating to others? Were you "on top" of this job or busy doing other things?
- Your employees
- Your equipment—wrong for the job.
- Your schedule—unreasonable and impossible.

Improving your financial image

Your financial image goes a long way towards enhancing your marketing efforts. Apart from your bidding procedures, negotiation skills, and ability to recognize contracting pitfalls, if your firm appears to be on firm financial footing, you'll be more attractive to purchasing agents than if you're not.

With the cost of making a sale to a new customer ranging above $2,000, your financial status most definitely affects your ability to market. Let's first look at potential sources of funds. Where can you get money to operate and market effectively to major corporations?

If your company is a sole proprietorship, you might use your own personal funds or opt for a bank loan, a loan from an individual, or a loan from or guaranteed by, a government agency. You might also consider a loan from another business. The amount of the loan you'll qualify for and the interest rate you must pay will largely be determined by your:

- track record;
- size of inventory;
- rate of inventory turnover;
- market potential; and
- profit potential.

A partnership has the same loan opportunities as a sole proprietorship with one more additional option: capital contributions by each partner. In addition to the sources listed previously, a corporation can also tap into:

- initial stockholders;
- equities—selling extra stock, common or preferred; and
- industrial revenue bonds.

Spell out your funding needs

Often, the larger the contract you win, the less likely you are able to sufficiently stock the required inventories and raw materials needed to complete the job. Most suppliers who undertake a large project or handle an unusually large amount of business experience financing problems. Only if you receive an equal volume of work each month and accounts receivable and payable are in perfect harmony, can you expect to finance a large inventory of raw materials primarily through internal cash flow.

As an alternative, you could try front-loaded contract billing or obtaining a revolving line of credit, thus maintaining a strong working capital position. If you decide to borrow money, there are two important concerns to consider: (1) What will the funds be used for? (2) What is the source of money for repayment? Short-term loans are usually repaid from the use of the current assets they have financed. Long-term loans are usually repaid from earnings.

Dealing with banks is precarious and requires planning and forethought, which most suppliers tend to ignore. This is unfortunate when you consider how closely marketing your business effectively is tied to your financial leverage. Try to establish an ongoing business relationship with a bank. Visit your banker, or a banker, and establish a rapport *before* you need a loan. The banker will then know you and your business and be more favorably disposed to grant you a loan when you actually need one. See Fig. 11-4.

Dealing with Banks

1. Show loyalty by dealing with one bank.

2. Savings:

   —Checking accounts
   —Loans

3. To enhance your chance of receiving a loan:

   A. Prepare a loan proposal that includes:

      —Amount of capital needed

Fig. 11-4. Quick tips for improving your banking relations.

—Type of loan—long- or short-term
—Terms secured, unsecured
—Proposed payback schedule

B. Clearly explain the purpose of the loan

C. Present company financial statements:

—Cash flow and pro forma projections
—balance sheets and income statements for three years
—Collateral
—Inventory
—Fixed assets
—Listing and aging of accounts receivable

D. Provide related nonfinancial information:

—Business strategy
—Data on company's industry
—Company's position in the industry
—List trade suppliers for references

4. Other Factors:

—Repay loans on time
—Make yourself known to bank officers well before you need a loan
—Bring in business for the bank
—Ask—the bank can't help you if it doesn't know your needs

Financial statements and your image

Are your financial statements audited by a certified public accountant (CPA)? This process serves as notice that your statements meet certain accounting tests and standards. Auditing lends credibility and professionalism to your financial statements, and the winners do it.

Audited statements present your company's financial data in a periodic, consistent, and acceptable fashion. They are important for marketing purposes because they present your company to outsiders in a professional way.

Audited statements are *your* statements. A CPA firm merely attests that "in its opinion, the financial statements fairly present the operations of your company for a given period of time, and the financial condition of your company at a given point in time."

Besides purchasing agents, many other people are favorably influenced by firms with audited financial statements. The following are five instances where having audited statements are beneficial:

1. *Banks.* Lending institutions are in business to make money, just like you. They do this by loaning money to sound investments. The bank seeks to determine the borrower's ability to repay in accordance with the terms of the loan. The banks are interested in a specified return for a given degree of risk. Because of market conditions or legal restrictions, banks frequently have a narrow range of possible return, but a broad range of prospective borrowers within that range.

   A bank can reduce its risk by being selective, provided it has enough competent data to make the decision. Banks also need sufficient information about the borrower to determine the degree of control or influence they want to impose via loan provisions. In the end, if a decision comes down to two apparent similar companies, one of which has audited statements, a banker will most likely put greater reliability on audited numbers because a professional independent agent was involved in reviewing their makeup.

2. *Bonding companies.* Those in the construction business know the importance of the bonding company. The larger your bonding capacity, the larger the jobs on which you can bid. Your financial statements play a significant part in getting the bonding capacity you desire, and these statements weigh heavily in the eyes of the bonding agent.

3. *State requirements.* In several states, incorporated businesses must annually file a certificate of condition. In some states, if a company's assets are over a certain amount, an independent auditor's statement is required.

4. *Selling a business and going public.* If you ever sell your business outright, or sell shares of the business, you must present a history of the firm to these potential investors, i.e., The Securities and Exchange Commission requires a five-year audited summary. Most buyers look askance at unaudited data.

5. *Creditor requirements.* Often, your suppliers might request financial information prior to extending credit. Depending on the size of the order and past experience, a supplier might require audited financial statements as opposed to in-house statements. One of the basic objectives of financial statements is to provide information that is useful for making economic decisions.

What do audits involve?

The focus of the auditor's examination is the financial statements of the company at their year-end date. The auditor must examine these financial statements and the underlying data, accounting records, and accounting systems that support those financial statements.

An audit team visits the company and tests the accounting records and its method of recording transactions. The key question is what are the internal controls and why are they necessary? The auditor reviews the transactions to see if they are properly recorded and executed within the existing system of procedures and controls.

After the auditor is satisfied that the internal accounting controls and procedures are working correctly, he examines the year-end statements. Through the use of third-party confirmations, the auditor can obtain independent support of cash balances (i.e., from banks), accounts receivable (i.e., from customers), and notes and accounts payable (from creditors). Through physical testing and observation, the auditor determines inventories and fixed assets. The auditor concludes the examination and issues one of several reports:

1. Unqualified; you pass with no problem!

2. Qualified Opinion; there were limitations in the scope of the audit, inconsistencies, or uncertainties.

3. Adverse Opinions; your financial statements deviate materially from generally accepted accounting procedure or there is inadequate disclosure.

4. Disclaimers of Opinion; there were obstacles limiting the auditors capability to render an opinion.

While the thought of having an audit might sound scary to you, it is actually a routine event with firms who successfully serve as key suppliers to large companies.

Exhibiting financial improvement

Even if you have had some lean years, your financial image should be presented as favorably as possible. If your firm has a steady rate of growth or an improving cash position, even if you might have a

_____Table 11-1._____
Horizontal Trend Analysis

Base year equals 100 percent; subsequent years are shown as percentages of the base-year figures. Example:

Balance Sheet

	Base Year	2nd Year	3rd Year
Total assets:	100%	105%	104%
Current	100	102	108
Fixed	100	98	99
Other	100	107	110
Total liabilities:	100	106	105
Short-term	100	102	101
Long-term	100	101	103
Net worth	100	101	104

Income Statement

	Base Year	2nd Year	3rd Year
Sales	100%	104%	109%
Cost of goods sold	100	102	111
Gross profit	100	102	98
Operating expenses	100	102	102
Net profit before taxes	100	101	100

long way to go before you can show a profit, emphasize the positive aspects of this improvement. Horizontal and vertical trend analysis are techniques you can use to present your financial image favorably. A sample trend analysis chart for balance sheets and income statements can be seen in Table 11-1.

With a horizontal trend analysis, you set all the components of your balance equal to 100 percent in the base year. Then, in succeeding years, you show change as it compares to the base year, i.e., no change would equal 100 percent. The same analysis can be applied to income statement components.

With vertical trend analysis for balance sheets, the figure for total assets each year is set equal 100 percent. Other balance sheet components are then expressed as percentages in comparison with total assets. See Table 11-2. For income statements, the analysis works the same way except "sales" are used in place of "assets." See Table 11-3.

_____Table 11-2._____
Vertical Trend Analysis

Total assets and total sales equal 100 percent, and the component entries are listed as percentage portions of those totals. Example:

Balance Sheet

		Base Year	2nd Year	3rd Year
Total assets (100%):		100%	100%	100%
Current	(Sums to 100%) {	14	11	8
Fixed		52	54	54
Other		34	35	38
Total liabilities:		106	104	101
Short-term	(Sums to 100%) {	36	33	32
Long-term		70	71	69
Net worth		−6	−4	−1

Income Statement

		Base Year	2nd Year	3rd Year
Sales (100%)		100%	100%	100%
Cost of goods sold	(Sums to 100%) {	79	79	80
Gross profit		21	21	20
Operating expenses		20	18	18
Net profit before taxes		1	3	2

_____Table 11-3._____
Income Statement

		Base Year	2nd Year	3rd Year
Sales (100%)		100%	100%	100%
Cost of Goods Sold		79%	79%	80%
	(Sums to 100%) {			
Gross Profit		21%	21%	20%
Operating Expenses		20%	18%	18%
Net Profit Before Taxes		1%	3%	2%

Strengthening your credit rating

Are you among the many businesses that could successfully market to large companies but never even try because of a poor credit rating? Suppose you've been in business for a few years, but only lately have had trouble meeting accounts payable. How can you keep your suppliers and creditors happy and position your company to have the appearance of financial solvency?

The best way for you to re-establish a good credit rating with your suppliers is to enclose a personal, detailed letter to each one with the next payment due. Your letter should explain the reasons for slow payment in the past and any other difficulties, and offer a brief synopsis of present operations. It should also thank the supplier for exhibiting patience and support, if applicable, with the assurance that every effort is being made, and will continue to be made, towards full payment and the development of a solid working relationship.

How the credit bureaus assess your business

Dun and Bradstreet, one of the world's largest credit rating agencies, examines several areas when making a credit evaluation:

- What is the character of principals, their reputation, and management ability? Are they conservative or venturesome? Do they seem intelligent? Do they have high living standards?

- Is the credit requested unreasonable or unusual for this type of business?

- What is the business location like, and what is the condition of the neighborhood?

- Is credit information readily furnished, and are answers direct and concise?

- Do the principals have other enterprises? Do they enhance the credit risk?

- How does the highest credit line extended to a customer compare with the present request under current business conditions?

- Is the business insurance adequate? Has a safety check been made to reduce fire hazards and other disasters?

Besides your level of cash, your accounts receivable and inventory are investigated in detail.

Deal honestly with credit bureaus as well as suppliers, avoiding claims that cannot be substantiated and commitments that cannot be met. When in doubt, follow the path of integrity. In the short run, you may take some knocks. In the long run, however, you'll always come out ahead. With suppliers, if your relationship has been honest, they can become valuable sources of short-term financing, via the extension of trade credit.

Seven golden rules

The following are seven golden rules to keep in mind as you begin your quest to become a corporate giant supplier:

1. Join associations. A primary rule for becoming a key supplier to corporate giants is to join associations composed of purchasing agents and other vendors. If you get no other benefit, your membership status will help mark your business as one of distinction.

2. Be flexible. The ability to be flexible is an essential element to successfully compete in our dynamic, technologically driven society. Before this century is over, the technology cycle might well be less than two years. Such rapid change will have a profound effect on individuals and their ability to keep pace in society. Such change also forebodes that an increasing array of opportunities awaits bold, innovative entrepreneurs.

3. Get to know the right people. One of the fastest ways to penetrate corporate giants is to identify the 10 or 15 people that you must know and meet them. Who are the 10 people you must know? They are different for everyone, but generally include the head of your industry's association, the director of key publications in your field, a banker, a few directors of a few target corporations, certainly a handful of key purchasing agents at target corporations, perhaps a management consultant or advisor, a Small Business Administration management assistance officer, a good graphics and design professional, and others.

4. Tie short-term objectives to long-term goals. Before taking on new tasks, carefully assess the long-term effects and potential. Never be forced to take on new jobs to pay the bills. Always assess a contract's potential for maintaining your working capital requirements and adding to your experience, track record, and capabilities.

5. Look for opportunities in adversity. The notion of looking for opportunities in adversity might sound like a platitude—it's not. Those who accept adversity as defeat, are defeated. Those who see adversity as a normal occurrence within the life of a business survive.

6. Simplify. Henry David Thoreau said it well and said it best more than 150 years ago. Our lives and our businesses are

"simply cluttered" with too many activities, and too many slips of paper, that simply don't support us.

7. Learn from your experiences. Learn from what went wrong and what went right, but invest in the future. You and your company are not just an extension of what came before today, because you have the ability to create. What products or services do you want to be offering a year from now? Three years from now? What profit level do you want to realize on the contracts you undertake? What do you want your image to be in the market place?

If you view your business and your marketing efforts as being inexorably tied to what came before, then all you have ever been is all you will ever be. How does the supplier who has never landed a contract with a corporate giant finally get one? Or examining the larger question, how do losers ever win? By going where they have never gone before. By doing what they fear. By doing what winners do.

Conclusion

The following is a list of 33 key points that were covered in *Selling to the Giants*. Keep it in a prominent place and read it often to remind you of what you need to be doing and what you'll want to plan for.

1. In the long run, your marketing effectiveness will live or die with your ability to delegate.

2. Virtually all businesses face the prospect of relocation in the first several years. It is a fact of business life. Face it and accept responsibility for maintaining accessibility.

3. If you are going to be calling on the "big boys," you will need a realistic perspective and approach. Recognize that you will never have all the time or money you need to take the big leap. Consequently, the time will never be exactly right. To put it another way, a good time to start is right *now*.

4. There are literally millions of vendors who could serve as suppliers to corporate giants but who continue to do nothing to further their opportunities or expose themselves to this market.

5. If it appears that everybody else maintains competitive advantages, fraught with key connections, ask yourself,

"Have I cut myself from the team or will I stick it out and play this season?" You won't find a single CEO among top companies who hasn't developed goals for the corporation. The mystery is why so many vendors operate without written, quantified goals.

6. If I got on a plane today and flew right to your plant or office and asked you to show me your marketing plan, could you?

7. You can be offering the greatest product or service in the world, but if you or your marketing staff haven't mastered the fundamentals of selling, your quest to successfully market to large corporations will be thwarted continuously.

8. Without the ability to close, your sales presentations will meander hopelessly. The sales that you make will represent a fraction of those that could be made by using proper closing techniques.

9. Stand your ground, even on the toughest sales calls. Your missionary efforts might ultimately yield a songbird that sings the praises of your products or services to others.

10. Perhaps the greatest lesson to be learned from the high cost of selling is the importance of working hard to keep the customer once your firm has landed the account.

11. Seeking new customers is time-consuming and essential. The continuous turnover of purchasing agents adds to the difficulty and costs of calling on large corporations.

12. You can bet the farm that corporate industry rivals try to learn as much about each other as possible.

13. Managing marketing is truly a never-ending task. There is always more to be done, new improvements to be made in presentations and supporting materials, new marketing leads to explore, and more follow-ups to be made.

14. One of the hallmarks in the evolution of a firm is when the entrepreneur recognizes that he/she must add a marketing manager because he can't do it all alone.

15. Successful firms are not overly reliant on a few large clients, but strive to achieve a balanced client mix instead.

16. Having the capabilities to successfully be a product or service vendor to large corporations is certainly a prerequi-

site for calling on them. However, you must be able to *document* your company's ability to do the job.

17. Purchasing has moved out of the corner of major corporations and into the mainstream. Top-level purchasing job appointments are going to people with broad experience. There is an evolution towards more entrepreneurial leadership—more decision making—closer to the everyday operating level.

18. Don't overlook the significant opportunities that trade shows can offer. It is an investment that can pay off in a big way. Corporate America meets at trade shows daily, and you should be there too.

19. Intense, expert, and comprehensive evaluation of suppliers continues to be a prime responsibility of purchasing agents.

20. Understanding how the world of the purchasing profession works is an important step on the road to marketing success with major corporations. If you can put yourself in the purchasing managers shoes, the trip can be a lot easier than you might expect. By reading what purchasing agents read, your company can get very close to the people who manage the business of buying goods and services for corporate giants.

21. A corporate suppliers guide can pack a lot of information into a small amount of space, saving both you and corporate purchasing departments time, money, and frustration.

22. There is no point and no advantage in beefing-up your credentials on vendor application forms. This tactic never works in the long run. Integrity does. Purchasing agents have "seen it all." Your best chance is to maintain 100 percent honesty.

23. Many suppliers, confronted with a first opportunity to do business with a big corporation, make the mistake of underbidding. This is because they have either not properly computed internal costs or hope to get a foot in the door. Either reason for underbidding is dangerous and leads to disastrous results.

24. Joining business associations and support groups will not, in and of itself, increase marketing effectiveness with corporate giants. Becoming an active member, however, can

add to your visibility, credibility, and highly professional image.

25. Never attempt to secure a contract by promising what you know you can't deliver. This is the quickest route back to marketing only to small businesses or the government.

26. Most entrepreneurs overlook, or worse, don't have the foresight, to prepare a counter proposal in advance. The vendor who comes to the negotiating table with a legitimate counter proposal has a feather in his cap.

27. When you suspect something is wrong in your relationship with a customer, it almost always is. What is the letter that you have to write? What is the phone call that you have to make? The one that you have been putting off.

28. Your financial image goes a long way towards enhancing your marketing efforts. All other things being equal, a vendor that appears to be on firm financial footing is more attractive to purchasing agents than one that is not.

29. When you read what your targets read, you begin to develop the ability to tap into the mind-set of those that can reward your firm with contracts.

30. Before this century is over, the technology cycle might well be less than two years. Such rapid change will have a profound effect on individuals and their ability to keep pace in society. Such change also forebodes an increasing array of opportunities, that await bold innovative entrepreneurs.

31. At some point in the growth and development of a company, all contracts undertaken should be carefully assessed for both long- and short-term contributions to the overall objectives of the firm.

32. Entrepreneurs can develop a greater sense of confidence by looking behind, above, beyond, and through adversity for the opportunity created as a by-product.

33. Entrepreneurism and adversity go hand in hand. Those who accept adversity as defeat, are defeated. Those who see adversity as a normal occurrence within the life of a business, survive. And those that view adversity as the flip side of opportunity, succeed.

Appendix A

Regional purchasing publications

The following is a list of regional publications for purchasing professionals.

Alabama Purchasor
P.O. Box 11506
Birmingham, AL 35202

Arizona Purchasor
Box 12715
Scottsdale, AZ 85267-2715

Chicago Purchasor
201 North Wells Street, #824
Chicago, IL 60606

Cincinnati Purchasor
P.O. Box 30376
Cincinnati, OH 45230

Columbia Area P.M.A.
c/o Bonded Scale and Machine
  Company
P.O. Box 27069
Columbus, OH 43227

*Empire Niagara Purchaser
  Professional*
1552 Hertel Avenue
Buffalo, NY 14216

Purchaser N.Y. State
1552 Hertel Avenue
Buffalo, NY 14216

Purchasing
1552 Hertel Avenue
Buffalo, NY 14216

Florida Purchaser
P.O. Box 1858
Jacksonville, FL 32201

Heart of America Purchaser
912 Baltimore Avenue, #900
Kansas City, MO 64105

Hoosier Purchaser
6100 Keystone Avenue
Indianapolis, IN 46220

Kentuckiana Purchasor
3415 Bardstown Road,
Box 35428
Louisville, KY 40218

Maryland Purchasing
1609 St. Paul
Baltimore, MD 21202

Metropolitan Purchasor
c/o White Eagle, Inc.
2550 Kuser Road
P.O. Box 8307
Trenton, NJ 08650

Mid-Atlantic Purchasing
7 Wesley Avenue
Glenside, PA 19038

Mid-South Purchaser
4023 Robins Drive
Jackson, MS 39206

Milwaukee Buylines
c/o Red Carpet Leisure
    Industries
4747 South Howell Avenue
Milwaukee, WI 53207

Midwest Purchasing
    Management
14 North 70th Avenue
St. Cloud, MN 56303

New England Purchaser
747 Main Street,
Concord, MA 01742

New Golden West Purchaser
c/o Illustrated Features
    Corporation
P.O. Box 4000
Palos Verdes Peninsula, CA 90274

Northwest Purchaser
P.O. Box 1293
Spokane, WA 99210

Orange Empire Purchasing
    Manager
1695 Crescent Street, #663
Anaheim, CA 92801

Oregon Purchaser
5331 Southwest Macadam, #224
Portland, OR 97201

Pacific Purchaser
819 S. Main Street
Burbank, CA 91506

St. Louis Purchaser
9701 Gravois Avenue
St. Louis, MO 63123

Note that *purchasor* and *purchaser* are apparently interchange-able.

Appendix B

Corporate purchasing contacts

The following are addresses of more than 200 corporate purchasing locations of major U.S. manufacturers and nonmanufacturers, alphabetized by state. Not all companies have centralized corporate purchasing departments, so some addresses represent branch purchasing locations.

Addresses change frequently, often by 20 percent every 12 months. Continual updating is necessary. The names, titles, addresses, and lists sorted by zip code for up to 15,000 buyers and purchasing executives nationwide is available for a fee from:

AMERICAN PURCHASING
  SOCIETY
11910 Oak Trail Way
Port Richey, FL 34668
(813) 862-7998

Alabama

VULCAN MATERIALS CO.
One Metroplex Dr.
Birmingham, AL 35209
(205) 877-3000

California

ATLANTIC RICHFIELD CO.
515 S. Flower St.
Los Angeles, CA 90071
(213) 486-3511

AVERY INTERNATIONAL
150 N. Orange Grove
   Blvd.
Pasadena, CA 91103
(818) 304-2000

CARNATION COMPANY
5045 Wilshire Blvd.
Los Angeles, CA 90036
(213) 932-6000

CONSOLIDATED
   FREIGHTWAYS
3240 Hillview Ave.
Palo Alto, CA 94303
(415) 326-1700

HEWLETT-PACKARD CORP.
3000 Hanover St.
Palo Alto, CA 94304
(415) 857-1501

HUGHES AIRCRAFT
   COMPANY
P.O. Box 45066
Los Angeles, CA 90045
(213) 568-7200

INTEL CORPORATION
3065 Bowers Ave.
Santa Clara, CA 95054
(408) 987-8080

KAISER ALUMINUM
   CORPORATION
300 Lakeside Dr.
Oakland, CA 94643
(415) 271-3057

LEVI STRAUSS & COMPANY
P.O. Box 7215
San Francisco, CA 94120
(415) 544-6637

LIQUID AIR CORPORATION
1 Embarcadero Center
San Francisco, CA 94111
(415) 765-4500

LITTON INDUSTRIES
360 N. Crescent Dr.
Beverly Hills, CA 90210
(213) 859-5000

LOCKHEAD AIRCRAFT CORP.
4500 Park Granada Blvd.
CalaBasas, CA 91399
(818) 712-2000

MEMOREX
1200 Memorex Dr.
Santa Clara, CA 95050
(408) 987-1000

NATIONAL SEMICONDUCTOR
2900 Semiconductor Dr.
Santa Clara, CA 95051
(408) 721-5000

NORTHROP CORPORATION
1840 Century Park E
Los Angeles, CA
  90067-2199
(213) 553-6262

ROCKWELL INTERNATIONAL
2230 E. Imperial Highway
El Segundo, CA 90245
(213) 647-5000

TELEDYNE INC.
1901 Ave. of the Stars
Los Angeles, CA
  90067-6046
(213) 277-3311

TRANSAMERICA INS. CORP.
  OF CA
1150 South Olive
Los Angeles, CA 90015
(213) 742-2111

VARIAN ASSOCIATES, INC.
611 Hansen Way, Bldg. 4A
Palo Alto, CA 94303
(414) 493-4000

Colorado

MONFORT INC.
P.O. Box G, 1930 AA St.
Greely, CO 80632
(303) 353-2311

Connecticut

CHAMPION INTERNATIONAL
  CORP.
1 Champion Plaza
Stamford, CT 06921
(203) 358-7000

COMBUSTION ENGINEERING
  INC.
900 Long Ridge Rd.
Stamford, CT 06904
(203) 329-8771

CONNECTICUT GENERAL
  LIFE INS.
900 Cottage Grove Rd.
Bloomfield, CT 06152
(203) 726-6000

CONNECTICUT MUTUAL LIFE
140 Garden St.
Hartford, CT 06154
(203) 727-6500

DEXTER CORPORATION
One Elm St.
Windsor Locks, CT 06096
(203) 627-9051

GENERAL ELECTRIC
  COMPANY
3135 Easton Turnpike
Fairfield, CT 06431
(203) 373-2211

GREAT NORTHERN NEKOOSA
  CORP.
401 Merritt, Ste. 7
Norwalk, CT 06856
(203) 845-9000

GTE SERVICE CORP.
One Stamford Forum
Stamford, CT 06904
(203) 965-2000

LONE STAR INDUSTRIES
One Greenwich Plaza, Box
   5050
Greenwich, CT 06836
(203) 661-3100

NORTHEAST UTILITIES
P.O. Box 270
Hartford, CT 06101
(203) 666-6911

OLIN CORP.
120 Long Ridge Rd.
Stamford, CT 06904-1355
(203) 356-2000

OTIS ELEVATOR COMPANY
10 Farm Springs Rd.
Farmington, CT 06032
(203) 674-4000

PERKIN-ELMER CORP.
761 Main Ave.
Norwalk, CT 06859
(203) 762-1000

PITNEY BOWES, INC.
Walter H. Wheeler Jr. Dr.
Stamford, CT 06926-0700
(203) 356-5000

SINGER COMPANY
8 Stamford Forum
Stamford, CT 06904
(203) 356-4200

STANLEY WORKS
1000 Stanley Dr.
New Britain, CT 06053
(203) 225-5111

THE TRAVELERS INSURANCE
   COMPANY
1 Tower Square
Hartford, CT 06183
(203) 227-0111

UNION CARBIDE
   CORPORATION
39 Old Ridgebury Rd.
Danbury, CT 06817
(203) 794-2000

UNIROYAL INC.
World Headquarters
Middlebury, CT 06749
(203) 573-2000

XEROX CORPORATION
Box 1600, Long Ridge Rd.
Stamford, CT 06904
(203) 968-3000

District of Columbia

USAIR
National Airport
Washington, DC 20001
(703) 892-7000

Florida

AUTOMATION INDUSTRIES
   INC.
Industrial Park
Fort Walton Beach, FL
   32548
(904) 244-7711

Georgia

COCA-COLA COMPANY
One Coca Cola Plaza, NW
Atlanta, GA 30313
(404) 676-2100

DELTA AIRLINES, INC.
Hartsfield Atlanta Int'l.
  Arpt.
Atlanta, GA 30320
(404) 765-2600

WEST POINT-PEPPERELL,
  INC.
P.O. Box 71
West Point, GA 31833
(404) 645-4000

Idaho

BOISE CASCADE CORP.
One Jefferson Sq.
Boise, ID 83728-0001
(208) 384-6161

Illinois

ABBOTT LABORATORIES
Abbott Park
N. Chicago, IL 60064
(708) 937-6100

ARCHER-DANIELS-MIDLAND
  CO.
4666 Faries Pkwy.
Decatur, IL 62525
(217) 424-5200

BEATRICE FOODS COMPANY
Two N. LaSalle St.
Chicago, IL 60602
(312) 558-4000

BELL & HOWELL COMPANY
5215 Old Orchard Rd.
Skokie, IL 60077
(708) 470-7100

BORG-WARNER
  CORPORATION
200 S. Michigan Ave.
Chicago, IL 60604
(312) 322-8500

COMMONWEALTH EDISON
  CO.
1 First National Plaza
Chicago, IL 60603
(312) 294-4321

FMC CORPORATION
200 East Randolph Dr.
Chicago, IL 60601
(312) 861-6000

HARTMARX CORPORATION
101 N. Wacker Dr.
Chicago, IL 60606
(312) 372-6300

INLAND STEEL INDUSTRIES
30 W. Monroe St.
Chicago, IL 60603
(312) 346-0300

KRAFT, INC.
Kraft Court
Glenview, IL 60025
(708) 998-2000

MOTOROLA, INC.
1303 E. Algonquin Rd.
Schaumburg, IL 60196
(708) 397-5000

NORTHERN TRUST CO.
50 S. LaSalle St.
Chicago, IL 60675
(312) 630-6000

QUAKER OATS COMPANY
N. Clark St., Quaker Tower
Chicago, IL 60610
(312) 222-7111

SANTA FE PACIFIC
224 S. Michigan Ave.
Chicago, IL 60604
(312) 786-6000

SEARS, ROEBUCK & COMPANY
Sears Tower
Chicago, IL 60684
(312) 875-2500

ZENITH ELECTRONICS CORP.
1000 Milwaukee Ave.
Glenview, IL 60025-2493
(708) 391-7000

Indiana

CENTRAL SOYA COMPANY,
   INC.
1300 Ft. Wayne Nt'l. Bank
   Bldg.
Fort Wayne, IN 46802
(219) 425-5100

CUMMINS ENGINE COMPANY,
   INC.
P.O. Box 3005
Columbus, IN 47202-3005
(812) 377-5000

NORTHERN INDIANA PUBLIC
   SERV.
5265 Hohman Ave.
Hammond, IN 46320
(219) 853-5200

Iowa

MAYTAG CORPORATION
403 W. 4th St., North
Newton, IA 50208
(515) 792-8000

Kansas

BEECH AIRCRAFT CORP.
P.O. Box 85
Wichita, KS 67201
(316) 681-7111

CESSNA AIRCRAFT COMPANY
P.O. Box 1521
Wichita, KS 67201
(316) 685-9111

Louisiana

MCDERMOTT, INC.
1010 Common St.
New Orleans, LA 70112
(504) 587-4411

Maryland

BLACK & DECKER MFG.
   COMPANY
701 E. Joppa Rd.
Towson, MD 21204
(301) 583-3900

MARRIOTT CORPORATION
10400 Fernwood Rd.
Bethesda, MD 20058
(301) 897-9000

MARTIN MARIETTA CORP.
6801 Rockledge Dr.
Bethesda, MD 20817
(301) 897-6000

Massachusetts

NORTON COMPANY
1 New Bond St.
Worcester, MA 01606
(508) 795-5000

POLAROID CORPORATION
549 Technology Sq.
Cambridge, MA 02139
(617) 577-2000

RAYTHEON COMPANY
141 Spring St.
Lexington, MA 02173
(617) 862-6600

THE GILLETTE COMPANY
Prudential Tower Bldg.
Boston, MA 02199
(617) 421-7000

WANG LABORATORIES INC.
1 Industrial Ave.
Lowell, MA 01851
(508) 459-5000

Michigan

AMERICAN MOTORS CORP.
27777 Franklin Rd.
Southfield, MI 48034
(313) 827-1000

CHRYSLER CORPORATION
12000 Chrysler Dr.
Highland Park, MI
   48288-1919
(313) 956-5252

CONSUMERS POWER CO.
212 W. Michigan Ave.
Jackson, MI 49201
(517) 788-0550

DOW CHEMICAL
2030 Willard H. Dow
   Center
Midland, MI 48674
(517) 636-1000

DOW CORNING
   CORPORATION
P.O. Box 994
Midland, MI 48686
(517) 496-4000

FEDERAL-MOGUL CORP.
26555 North Western Hwy.
Southfield, MI 48034
(313) 354-7700

FORD MOTOR COMPANY
The American Rd.
Dearborn, MI 48121
(313) 322-3000

GENERAL MOTORS
   CORPORATION
3044 W. Grand Blvd.
Detroit, MI 48202
(313) 556-5000

KELLOGG COMPANY
One Kellogg Sq., Box 3599
Battle Creek, MI
   49016-3599
(616) 961-2000

MICHIGAN CONSOLIDATED
   GAS CO.
500 Griswold
Detroit, MI 48226
(313) 965-2430

THE UPJOHN COMPANY
7000 Portage Rd.
Kalamazoo, MI 49001
(616) 323-4000

WHIRLPOOL CORPORATION
2000 M-63
Benton Harbor, MI
   49022-2692
(616) 926-5000

Minnesota

BEMIS COMPANY
625 Marquette Ave.
Minneapolis, MN 55402
(612) 340-6000

CONTROL DATA
   CORPORATION
8100 34th Ave., S
Minneapolis, MN 55440
(612) 853-8100

GENERAL MILLS, INC.
P.O. Box 1113
Minneapolis, MN 55440
(612) 540-2311

HONEYWELL, INC.
Honeywell Plaza
Minneapolis, MN 55408
(612) 870-5200

INTERNATIONAL
   MULTIFOODS CORP.
Multifoods Tower,
Box 2942
Minneapolis, MN 55402
(612) 340-3300

NORTHERN STATES POWER
   CO.
414 Nicollet Mall
Minneapolis, MN 55401
(612) 330-5500

PILLSBURY CENTER
200 S. 6th St.
Minneapolis, MN 55402
(612) 330-4966

Missouri

ANHEUSER-BUSCH COMPANY
One Busch Place
St. Louis, MO 63118
(314) 577-2000

CONSOLIDATED ALUMINUM
63146 Westline Ind. Dr.
St. Louis, MO 63141
(314) 878-6950

GENERAL DYNAMICS
   CORPORATION
Pierre Laclede Center
St. Louis, MO 6105-1861
(314) 889-8200

MAY DEPARTMENT STORES
611 Olive St.
St. Louis, MO 63101
(314) 342-6300

McDonnell Douglas
  Corp.
P.O. Box 516
St. Louis, MO 63166
(314) 232-0232

Monsanto Corporation
800 N. Lindbergh
St. Louis, MO 63167
(314) 694-1000

Southwestern Bell
  Telephone Co.
1010 Pine St.
St. Louis, MO 63101
(314) 235-9800

Nebraska

Conagra
One Central Park Plaza
Omaha, NE 68102
(402) 978-4000

New Hampshire

Micro-Precision Co.
Main St.
Sunapee, NH 03782
(603) 763-2394

New Jersey

America Cyanamid
  Company
One Cyanamid Plaza
Wayne, NJ 07470
(201) 831-2000

Armco Inc.
300 Interpace Pkwy.
Parsippany, NJ 07054
(201) 316-5200

AT&T Technologies
One Oak Way
Berkeley Heights, NJ
  07922
(908) 771-2000

Campbell Soup Company
Campbell Place
Camden, NJ 08101
(609) 342-4800

GAF Corporation
1361 Alps Rd.
Wayne, NJ 07470
(201) 628-3000

Ingersoll-Rand Company
200 Chestnut Ridge Rd.
Woodcliff Lake, NJ 07675
(201) 573-0123

Merck & Co., Inc.
P.O. Box 2000
Rahway, NJ 07065
(201) 574-4000

Squibb Corp.
P.O. Box 4000
Princeton, NJ 08543
(609) 921-4000

Warner-Lamber Company
201 Tabor Rd.
Morris Plains, NJ 07950
(201) 540-2000

New York

Amax, Inc.
200 Park Ave.
New York, NY 10166
(212) 856-4200

Amstar Corporation
1251 Ave. of the Americas
New York, NY 10020
(212) 489-9000

Asarco, Inc.
180 Maiden Lane
New York, NY 10038
(212) 510-1800

Avnet
80 Cutter Mill Rd.
Great Neck, NY 10021
(516) 466-7000

Avon Products Inc.
9 S. 57th St.
New York, NY 10019
(212) 546-6015

Bausch & Lomb
One Lincoln First Sq., Box
   54
Rochester, NY 14601-0054
(716) 338-6000

Bristol-Myers Squibb Co.
345 Park Ave.
New York, NY 10154
(212) 808-6000

Carrier Corporation
Bldg. TR4, Door 25 Carrier
   Pkwy.
Syracuse, NY 13221
(315) 432-6000

Colgate-Palmolive
   Company
300 Park Avenue
New York, NY 10022
(212) 310-2000

Con Edison Co. of NY
4 Irving Place
New York, NY 10003
(212) 460-4600

Corning Glass Works
Houghton Park
Corning, NY 14831
(607) 974-9000

Crouse-Hinds
P.O. Box 4999
Syracuse, NY 13221
(315) 477-7000

Eastman Kodak Company
343 State St.
Rochester, NY 14650
(716) 724-4000

F. W. Woolworth
   Company
233 Broadway
New York, NY 10279
(212) 553-2000

Grumman Corporation
1111 Stewart Ave.
Bethpage, NY 11714
(516) 575-0574

IBM Corporation
Old Orchard Rd.
Armonk, NY 10504
(914) 765-1900

ITT Corporation
320 Park Ave.
New York, NY 10022
(212) 752-6000

JOHNSON & JOHNSON
Johnson & Johnson Plaza
New Brunswick, NY 08903
(201) 524-0400

JOSEPH SEAGRAM & SONS
375 Park Ave.
New York, NY 10152
(212) 572-7000

J. P. STEVENS & COMPANY
1185 Ave. of the Americas
New York, NY 10036
(212) 930-2000

MANUFACTURERS HANOVER
  TRUST CO.
270 Park Ave.
New York, NY 10017
(212) 286-6000

MARINE MIDLAND BANK,
  N.A.
1 Marine Midland Center
Buffalo, NY 14240
(716) 843-2424

McGRAW-HILL, INC.
1221 Avenue of the
  Americas
New York, NY 10020
(212) 512-2000

METROPOLITIAN LIFE
  INSURANCE
1 Madison Ave.
New York, NY 10010
(212) 578-2211

NEW YORK AIR BRAKE CO.
Starbuck Avenue
Watertown, NY 13601
(315) 782-7000

NEW YORK LIFE INSURANCE
51 Madison Ave.
New York, NY 10010
(212) 576-7000

NIAGARA MOHAWK POWER
  CORP.
300 Erie Blvd. W
Syracuse, NY 13202
(315) 474-1511

NORTH AMERICAN PHILIPS
  CO.
100 E. 42nd St.
New York, NY 10017
(212) 697-3600

PFIZER INC.
235 E. 42nd St.
New York, NY 10017
(212) 573-2323

PHILIP MORRIS, INC.
120 Park Ave.
New York, NY 10017
(212) 880-5000

OGDEN CORPORATION
2 Pennsylvania Plaza
New York, NY 10121
(212) 868-6100

REVLON, INC.
767 Fifth Ave.
New York, NY 10153
(212) 572-5000

SCOVILL INC.
499 Park Ave.
New York, NY 10022
(212) 750-0200

SPERRY & HUTCHINSON
  COMPANY
330 Madison Ave., 7th Fl.
New York, NY 10017
(212) 986-8610

WESTVACO CORPORATION
299 Park Ave.
New York, NY 10171
(212) 688-5000

W.R. GRACE & COMPANY
1114 Ave. of the Americas
New York, NY 10036
(212) 819-5500

TIME WARNER INC.
Time & Life Bldg.
New York, NY 10020
(212) 522-1212

North Carolina

BLUE BELL, INC.
301 N. Elm St.
Greensboro, NC 27401
(919) 373-3400

BURLINGTON INDUSTRIES
P.O. Box 21207
Greensboro, NC 27420
(919) 379-2000

CONE MILLS CORP.
1201 Maple St.
Greensboro, NC 27405
(919) 379-6220

Ohio

ANCHOR HOCKING
  CORPORATION
109 N. Broad St.
Lancaster, OH 43132
(614) 687-2111

B. F. GOODRICH COMPANY
3925 Embassy Pkwy.
Akron, OH 44313
(216) 374-2000

BORDEN PACKAGING & IND.
180 E. Broad St., 31st Fl.
Columbus, OH 43215
(614) 225-4000

CHAMPION SPARK PLUG
  COMPANY
P.O. Box 910
Toledo, OH 43661-0001
(419) 535-2567

CINCINNATI MILACRON INC.
4701 Marburg Ave.
Cincinnati, OH 45209
(513) 841-8100

DANA CORPORATION
P.O. Box 1000
Toledo, OH 43697
(419) 535-4500

EATON CORPORATION
1111 Superior Ave., NE
Cleveland, OH 44114
(216) 523-5000

FEDERATED DEPARTMENT
   STORES
7 W. Seventh St.
Cincinnati, OH 45202
(513) 579-7000

GOODYEAR TIRE & RUBBER
   CO.
1144 E. Market St.
Akron, OH 44316
(216) 796-2121

GOULD, INC.
35129 Curtis Blvd.
East Lake, OH 44094
(216) 953-5000

LIBBEY-OWENS-FORD
   COMPANY
811 Madison Ave.
Toledo, OH 43695
(419) 247-3731

MARATHON OIL COMPANY
539 S. Main St.
Findlay, OH 45840
(419) 422-2121

MEAD CORP.
Courthouse Plaza, NE
Dayton, OH 45463
(513) 222-6323

METAL FORGE
291 Marconi Blvd.
Columbus, OH 43215
(614) 224-2271

NCR CORPORATION
Technical Systems Div.
Dayton, OH 45479
(513) 445-5000

NATIONWIDE INSURANCE
One Nationwide Plaza
Columbus, OH 43216
(614) 249-7111

OWENS CORNING
   FIBERGLASS CORP.
Fiberglass Tower
Toledo, OH 43659
(419) 248-8000

PROCTOR & GAMBLE
   COMPANY
1 Proctor & Gamble Plaza
Cincinnati, OH 45202
(513) 983-1100

SHERWIN WILLIAMS
   COMPANY
101 Prospect Ave., NW
Cleveland, OH 44115
(216) 566-2000

TRW, INC.
1900 Richmond Rd.
Cleveland, OH 44124
(216) 291-7000

UNITED BRANDS COMPANY
One E. Fourth St.
Cincinnati, OH 45202
(513) 579-2115

Oregon

LOUISIANA-PACIFIC CORP.
111 S.W. Fifth Ave.
Portland, OR 97204
(503) 221-0800

TEKTRONIX, INC.
P.O. Box 500
Beaverton, OR 97077
(503) 627-7111

Pennsylvania

AIR PRODUCTS & CHEMICALS
    INC.
P.O. Box 538
Allentown, PA 18105
(215) 481-4911

ARMSTRONG WORLD
    INDUSTRIES
P.O. Box 3001, Lancaster Sq.
Lancaster, PA 17604
(717) 397-0611

BETHLEHEM STEEL
    CORPORATION
8th & Eaton Ave., Martin
    Tower
Bethlehem, PA 18016
(215) 694-2424

CONSOLIDATED NATURAL
    GAS SERVICE
CNG Tower, 4 Gateway
    Ctr.
Pittsburgh, PA 15222
(412) 227-1200

CONSOLIDATED RAIL CORP.
6 Penn Center Plaza
Philadelphia, PA 19103
(215) 977-4000

KOPPERS COMPANY INC.
801 Koppers Bldg.
Pittsburgh, PA 15219
(412) 227-2773

McGRAW EDISON CO.
P.O. Box 2850
Pittsburgh, PA 15230
(412) 777-3200

MELLON BANK, N.A.
Mellon Square
Pittsburgh, PA 15258
(412) 234-5000

PENWALT CORPORATION
3 Parkway
Philadelphia, PA 19102
(215) 587-7000

PPG INDUSTRIES
One PPG Place
Pittsburgh, PA 15272
(412) 434-3131

SCOTT PAPER COMPANY
Scott Plaza
Philadelphia, PA 19113
(215) 522-5000

SMITH KLINE & FRENCH
1500 Spring Garden St.
Philadelphia, PA 19101
(215) 751-4000

SUNBEAM CORPORATION
Two Oliver Plaza, Box 456
Pittsburgh, PA 15230
(412) 562-4000

WESTINGHOUSE ELECTRIC
    CORP.
6 Gateway Center
Pittsburgh, PA 15222
(412) 244-2000

Puerto Rico

ST. REGIS PAPER COMPANY
A St., Reparada Ind.
   Development
Ponce, Puerto Rico
(809) 844-8845

Tennessee

GENESCO, INC.
Genesco Park
Nashville, TN 37202
(615) 367-7000

NORTHERN TELECOM INC.
200 Athens Way
Nashville, TN 37228
(615) 734-4000

Texas

AMERICAN PETROFINA
P.O. Box 2159
Dallas, TX 75221
(214) 750-2400

BIG THREE INDUSTRIES
P.O. Box 3047
Houston, TX 77253
(713) 868-0333

CONOCO INC.
600 N. Dairy Ashford Rd.
Houston, TX 77079
(713) 293-1000

EXXON COMPANY
P.O. Box 2812
Houston, TX 77001
(713) 676-3636

KIMBERLY CLARK CORP.
DFW Airport, Box 619100
Dallas, TX 75261
(214) 830-1200

PENNZOIL COMPANY
P.O. Box 2967
Houston, TX 77252-2967
(713) 546-4000

ROCKWELL INTERNATIONAL
P.O. Box 10462
Dallas, TX 75207
(214) 996-5000

TANDY CORP./RADIO SHACK
1800 One Tandy Center
Ft. Worth, TX 76102
(817) 390-3700

TENNECO OIL COMPANY
P.O. Box 2511
Houston, TX 77001
(713) 757-2131

TEXAS INSTRUMENTS INC.
P.O. Box 655474
Dallas, TX 75265
(214) 995-2011

THE SOUTHLAND CORP.
2828 N. Haskell Ave.
Dallas, TX 75221
(214) 828-7011

Virginia

FAIRCHILD INDUSTRIES
300 W. Service Rd., Box
   10803
Chantilly, VA 22021
(703) 478-5800

NORFOLK & WESTERN RY
Three Commercial Pl.
Norfolk, VA 23510
(804) 629-2682

Washington

BOEING COMPANY
7755 E. Marginal Way
Seattle, WA 98108
(206) 656-2121

PACCAR
P.O. Box 1518
Bellevue, WA 98009
(206) 455-7400

TODD SHIPYARDS
  CORPORATION
1102 S.W. Massachusetts
Seattle, WA 98134
(206) 223-1560

WEYERHAEUSER COMPANY
Corp. Headquarters
Tacoma, WA 98477
(206) 924-2345

Wisconsin

CONSOLIDATED PAPERS, INC.
P.O. Box 50
Wisconsin Rapids, WI
  54494
(715) 422-3111

NORTHWESTERN MUTUAL
  LIFE INS.
720 E. Wisconsin Ave.
Milwaukee, WI 53202
(414) 271-1444

REXNORD CORPORATION
350 N. Sunny Slope
Brookfield, WI 53005
(414) 797-6900

Appendix C

Association and convention sources

The following is a state sampling of convention and visitors bureaus, listed alphabetically. There is also a list of trade show directories and other sources.

Alabama

GREATER BIRMINGHAM
  CONVENTION AND
  VISITORS BUREAU
2027 1st Avenue North
Suite 300
Birmingham, AL 35203
(205) 252-9825

Alaska

ANCHORAGE CONVENTION
  AND VISITORS BUREAU
1600 A St.
Anchorage, AK 99501
(907) 276-4118

Arizona

PHOENIX AND VALLEY OF THE SUN
  CONVENTION AND
  VISITORS BUREAU
505 North 2nd Street, Suite 300
Phoenix, AZ 85004
(602) 254-6500

California

PASADENA CONVENTION
  AND VISITORS BUREAU
171 South Los Robles
Pasadena, CA 91101
(818) 795-9311

SAN DIEGO CONVENTION
  AND VISITORS BUREAU
1200 3rd Avenue, Suite 824
San Diego, CA 92101
(619) 232-3101

SAN FRANCISCO CONVENTION
  AND VISITORS BUREAU
201 3rd Street, #900
San Francisco, CA 94103
(415) 974-6900

Colorado

DENVER AND COLORADO
  CONVENTION AND
  VISITORS BUREAU
225 West Colfax Avenue
Denver, CO 80202
(303) 892-1112

Connecticut

GREATER HARTFORD
  CONVENTION AND
  VISITORS BUREAU, INC.
1 Civic Center Plaza
Hartford, CT 06103
(203) 728-6789

District of Columbia

WASHINGTON CONVENTION
  AND VISITORS ASSOCIATION,
  INC.
1212 New York Ave., NW
Sixth Floor
Washington, DC 20005
(202) 789-7000

Florida

GREATER MIAMI CONVENTION
  AND VISITORS BUREAU
701 Brickell Ave.
Suite 2700
Miami, FL 33131
(305) 539-3000

TAMPA/HILLSBOROUGH
  CONVENTION AND VISITORS
  ASSOCIATION, INC.
111 Madison Street
Suite 1010
Tampa, FL 33602
(813) 223-1111

Georgia

ATLANTA CONVENTION
  AND VISITORS BUREAU
233 Peachtree Street, N.E.
Suite #2000
Atlanta, GA 30303
(404) 521-6600

Hawaii

HAWAII VISITORS BUREAU
2270 Kalakaua Avenue
  Suite 801
Honolulu, HI 96815
(808) 923-1811

Illinois

CHICAGO CONVENTION
  AND TOURISM BUREAU, INC.
McCormick Place on the Lake
Chicago, IL 60616
(312) 567-8500

Indiana

INDIANAPOLIS CONVENTION
   AND VISITORS ASSOCIATION
1 Hoosier Dome, Suite 100
200 South Capitol Avenue
Indianapolis, IN 46225
(317) 639-4282

Iowa

IOWA CITY/CORALVILLE
   CONVENTION AND
   VISITORS BUREAU, INC.
325 E. Washington St.
P.O. Box 2358
Des Moines, IA 52244
(319) 337-6592

Kansas

WICHITA CONVENTION
   AND VISITORS BUREAU
100 S. Main St., Suite 100
Wichita, KS 67202
(316) 265-2800

Kentucky

GREATER LEXINGTON
   CONVENTION AND
   VISITORS BUREAU
430 West Vine Street, Suite 363
Lexington, KY 40507
(606) 233-1221

LOUISVILLE CONVENTION
   AND VISITORS BUREAU
400 S. First
Louisville, KY 40202
(502) 584-2121

Louisiana

GREATER NEW ORLEANS TOURIST
   AND CONVENTION COMMISSION
1520 Sugar Bowl Drive
New Orleans, LA 70112
(504) 566-5011

Maine

CONVENTION AND VISITORS
   BUREAU OF GREATER
   PORTLAND
142 Free Street
Portland, ME 04101
(207) 772-4994

Maryland

BALTIMORE CONVENTION BUREAU
1 East Pratt Street, Plaza Level
Baltimore, MD 21202
(301) 659-7300

Massachusetts

GREATER BOSTON CONVENTION
   AND VISITORS BUREAU
800 Boylston St.
P.O. Box 490
Boston, MA 02199
(617) 536-4100

Michigan

METROPOLITAN DETROIT
   CONVENTION AND
   VISITORS BUREAU
100 Renaissance Center,
   Suite 1950
Detroit, MI 48243
(313) 259-4333

Minnesota

MINNEAPOLIS CONVENTION
  AND VISITORS COMMISSION
1219 Marquette Ave.
Minneapolis, MN 55403
(612) 348-4313

Mississippi

JACKSON CONVENTION
  AND VISITORS BUREAU
109 W. Washington Ave.
Jackson, MS 49201
(517) 783-3330

Missouri

CONVENTION AND VISITORS
  BUREAU OF GREATER
  KANSAS CITY
1100 Main Street, Suite 2550
Kansas City, MO 64105
(816) 221-5242

ST. LOUIS CONVENTION AND
  VISITORS COMMISSION
10 South Broadway, Suite 300
St. Louis, MO 63102
(314) 421-1023

Nebraska

LINCOLN CONVENTION
  AND VISITORS BUREAU
1221 N. Street, Suite 320
Lincoln, NE 68508
(402) 476-7511

Nevada

LAS VEGAS CONVENTION
  AND VISITORS AUTHORITY
3150 Paradise Road
Las Vegas, NV 89109-9096
(702) 733-2323

New Jersey

ATLANTIC CITY CONVENTION
  AND VISITORS BUREAU
2314 Pacific Ave.
Atlantic City, NJ 08401
(609) 348-7100

New Mexico

ALBUQUERQUE CONVENTION
  AND VISITORS BUREAU, INC.
625 Silver St. SW, Suite 210
P.O. Box 26866
Albuquerque, NM 87125
(505) 842-9918

New York

ALBANY COUNTY CONVENTION
  AND VISITORS BUREAU
52 S. Pearl St.
Albany, NY 12207
(518) 434-1217

BUFFALO AREA CHAMBER OF
  COMMERCE CONVENTION
  AND TOURISM DIVISION
107 Delaware Avenue
Buffalo, NY 14202
(716) 852-0511

NEW YORK CONVENTION
  AND VISITORS BUREAU
2 Columbus Circle
New York, NY 10019
(212) 397-8200

North Carolina

CHARLOTTE CONVENTION
  AND VISITORS BUREAU, INC.
229 N. Church St.
Charlotte, NC 28202
(704) 334-CCVB

WINSTON-SALEM CONVENTION
  AND VISITORS BUREAU
  GREATER WINSTON-SALEM
  CHAMBER OF COMMERCE
500 W. 5th St.
P.O. Box 1408
Winston-Salem, NC 27102-1408
(919) 725-2361

Ohio

GREATER CINCINNATI
  CONVENTION AND
  VISITORS BUREAU
300 W. 6th St.
Cincinnati, OH 45202
(513) 621-2142

CONVENTION AND VISITORS
  BUREAU OF GREATER
  CLEVELAND
3100 Tower City Center
Cleveland, OH 44113
(216) 621-4110

Oklahoma

OKLAHOMA CITY CONVENTION
  AND TOURISM BUREAU
4 Santa Fe Plaza
Oklahoma City, OK 73102
(405) 278-8912

TULSA CONVENTION
  AND VISITORS BUREAU
616 South Boston
Tulsa, OK 74119
(918) 585-1201

Oregon

GREATER PORTLAND
  CONVENTION AND VISITORS
  ASSOCIATION, INC.
26 Southwest Salmon
Portland, OR 97204-3299
(503) 222-2223

Pennsylvania

PHILADELPHIA CONVENTION
  AND VISITORS BUREAU
1515 Market St., Suite 2020
Philadelphia, PA 19102
(215) 636-3300

PITTSBURGH CONVENTION
  AND VISITORS BUREAU
4 Gateway Center
Pittsburgh, PA 15222
(412) 281-7711

Rhode Island

GREATER PROVIDENCE
  CONVENTION AND
  VISITORS BUREAU
Commerce Center
30 Exchange Terrace
Providence, RI 02903
(401) 274-1636

South Carolina

CHARLESTON/TRIDENT
  CONVENTION AND
  VISITORS BUREAU
P.O. Box 975
Charleston, SC 29402
(803) 577-2510

South Dakota

RAPID CITY CONVENTION
    AND VISITORS BUREAU
P.O. Box 747
Rapid City, SD 57709
(605) 343-1744

Tennessee

CHATTANOOGA AREA
    CONVENTION AND
    VISITORS BUREAU
1001 Market Street
Chattanooga, TN 37402
(615) 756-8687

MEMPHIS CONVENTION
    AND VISITORS BUREAU
50 N. Front St., Suite 450
Memphis, TN 38103
(901) 576-8181

Convention and Visitors
    DIVISION NASHVILLE AREA
    CHAMBER OF COMMERCE
161 4th Avenue, North
Nashville, TN 37219
(615) 259-3900

Texas

DALLAS CONVENTION
    AND VISITORS BUREAU
1201 Elm St., Suite 2000
Dallas, TX 75270
(214) 746-6677

GREATER HOUSTON CONVENTION
    AND VISITORS COUNCIL
3300 Main Street
Houston, TX 77002
(713) 523-5050

SAN ANTONIO CONVENTION
    AND VISITORS BUREAU
P.O. Box 839966
San Antonio, TX 78283
(512) 270-8700

Utah

SALT LAKE CITY CONVENTION
    AND VISITORS BUREAU
180 South West Temple
Salt Lake City, UT 84101-1493
(801) 521-2822

Virginia

METROPOLITAN RICHMOND
    CONVENTION AND
    VISITORS BUREAU
300 East Main Street, Suite 100
Richmond, VA 23219
(804) 782-2777

VIRGINIA BEACH
    CONVENTION BUREAU
P.O. Box 89
Virginia Beach, VA 23458
(804) 428-8000

Washington

SEATTLE/KING COUNTY
    CONVENTION AND
    VISITORS BUREAU
520 Pike St., Suite 1300
Seattle, WA 98101
(206) 461-5800

West Virginia

CHARLESTON CONVENTION
    AND VISITORS BUREAU
200 Civic Center Drive
Charleston, WV 25301
(304) 344-5075

Wisconsin

GREEN BAY AREA VISITORS AND
  CONVENTION BUREAU, INC.
1901 South Oneida Street
P.O. Box 10596
Green Bay, WI 54307-0596
(414) 494-9507

GREATER MILWAUKEE
  CONVENTION AND
  VISITORS BUREAU
756 North Milwaukee Street
Milwaukee, WI 53202
(414) 273-3950

The following is a list of trade show directories available for a small fee or through your local library.

Directory of Conventions
Research Department
Successful Meetings
633 Third Avenue
New York, NY 10017
(212) 986-4800

Annual listing of conventions by geographic area. Contains a key word index by industry group or interest.

Trade Shows and Professional
  Exhibits Directory
  Gale Research Inc.
Book Tower
Detroit, MI 48226
(313) 961-2242

Lists more than 2,100 scheduled exhibitions, trade shows, association conventions, and other sales events by subject. Provides types of audience, anticipated attendance, and display prices.

National Trade and Professional
Associations
Columbia Books, Inc.
1212 New York Avenue, NW, #330
Washington, DC 20005
(202) 898-0662

Lists annual meeting or convention dates and locations for each association. Geographic, subject (key word), and budget index.

Tradeshow Week Data Book
12233 W. Olympic Blvd., #236
Los Angeles, CA 90064
(213) 826-5696

Published annually by the Tradeshow Bureau. Features marketing
and statistical data on more than 5,000 trade shows.

Other sources

Tradeshow Week
Tradeshow Week, Inc.
12233 W. Olympic Blvd., #236
Los Angeles, CA 90064
(213) 826-5696

Lists trade shows scheduled for the week six months in advance.
Includes location, contact name, address, phone number, pro-
jected square footage of exhibit space, number of booths, number of exhibiting companies, and expected attendance.

Special Events Reports
Special Events Reports, Inc.
213 West Institute Place, #303
Chicago, IL 60610
(312) 944-1727

Biweekly international newsletter on events, festivals, and promotions.

INTERNATIONAL ASSOCIATION OF
    CONVENTION AND VISITORS' BUREAUS
Box 758
Champaign, IL 61820
(217) 359-8881

INTERNATIONAL EXHIBITORS' ASSOCIATION
5501 Backlick Road, #200
Springfield, VA 22050
(703) 941-3725

AMERICAN SOCIETY OF ASSOCIATION
EXECUTIVES
1575 Eye Street, NW
Washington, DC 20005
(202) 626-2723

Produces a calendar of various programs of affiliated societies which might provide information on trade shows and meetings.

Appendix D

Professional associations

These are several, well-known business associations and advocacy support groups that can add to your overall visibility that you might want to learn about. Joining any of these organizations will not, in and of itself, increase your effectiveness in marketing to the giants, however, each group provides unique benefits.

CHAMBER OF COMMERCE OF
  THE UNITED STATES
1615 H. St., NW
Washington, DC 20062
(202) 659-6000

The U.S. Chamber of Commerce is organized on three levels. local, state, and national. On the national level, the Chamber of Commerce works with developing local and state chambers and represents national business interests to the federal government.

State chambers coordinate local chamber programs and represent the state business community to the state government. Information on small business programs in the state is available through the state chamber.

Local chambers serve the local business community with programs in economic development, community and human resources, and public affairs. Programs might include:

- small business development
- group and individual counseling on business problems
- group seminars on management
- start-up assistance, lending, and equity capital programs

The Chamber's Small Business Programs Office serves as a central clearinghouse for information on getting started in business, expanding your business overseas, and managing your business. Two information sources include:

1. The *Information Resources Guide*, a list of U.S. Chamber publications, guides, and videos.
2. The *State and Local Chamber List*, a complete list of state and local chambers that have small business and export assistance programs.

You can also consult with chamber staff specialists who provide information, opinions, and analysis to small businesses by calling (301) 468-5128 and asking for the U.S. Chamber Staff Specialists' brochure. Once obtaining the brochure, you can select the appropriate specialist to help you.

THE NATIONAL FEDERATION OF
 INDEPENDENT BUSINESS (NFIB)
Headquarters:
150 West 20th Ave.
San Mateo, CA 94403
(415) 341-7441

600 Maryland Ave., SW, Suite 700
Washington, DC 20024
(202) 554-9000

The NFIB represents more than 500,000 business owners in the legislatures as well as with state and federal agencies and is the nation's largest organization representing small and independent businesses. NFIB also offers information on free enterprise, entrepreneurship, and small business, as well as providing surveys on economic trends. It also lobbies for members on particular issues.

NATIONAL SMALL BUSINESS
  ASSOCIATION (NSBA)
1604 K. St., NW
Washington, DC 20006
(202) 293-8830

The NSBA is a membership-based association of business owners representing all types of businesses. The NSBA presents small
businesses' point of view to all levels of government and the Congress and develops programs of national policy that are of concern
to the small business community.

Key services include providing members with a monthly
newsletter and other materials that keep them up-to-date on issues
affecting their businesses and alerting members to federal contracting opportunities through the Bidder's Early Alert Message system.

NATIONAL ASSOCIATION OF
  MANUFACTURERS (NAM)
1331 Pennsylvania Ave., NW, #1500N
Washington, DC 20004
(202) 637-3000

The NAM, a group widely recognized by large corporations,
consist of 15,000 manufacturing firms, with more than 75 percent
having fewer than 500 employees. Member firms account for 80
percent of the nation's industrial capacity. NAM is a strong voice
for the manufacturing community in Washington. It provides
members with an opportunity to participate in the public policy
process through membership of 14 policy committees. Major subject areas include:

- Resource and technology—energy, environment, innovation, and natural resources.

- International economic affairs—international investment, finance, and trade.

- Industrial relations—labor relations, human resources, em-
  ployee benefits, loss prevention, and control.

- Government regulation, competition, and small manufacturing.

- Taxation and fiscal policy.

NAM services include a roster of 100 subject specialists including legislative specialists, lawyers, communications advisors, and public affairs experts who help members with questions and problems. The NAM Member Service Guide provides the names and telephone numbers of these specialists. Also, *Enterprise*, NAM's monthly magazine, focuses on emerging issues.

NATIONAL ASSOCIATION OF WOMEN
  BUSINESS OWNERS (NAWBO)
600 S. Federal Street, #400
Chicago, IL 60605
(312) 922-0465

The NAWBO consists of dozens of local chapters and several thousand members nationwide. NAWBO helps female business owners expand their operations and represents female business interests to federal and state governments.

NAWBO services include providing counseling and technical assistance at the local level, primarily through networking with local members, holding monthly programs at the local chapters, which address female business-owner problems, and sponsoring an annual national conference that offers management and technical assistance training through workshops and seminars.

NATIONAL SMALL BUSINESS UNITED (NSBU)
1155 15th Street, NW, #710
Washington, DC 20005
(800) 345-NSBU

The SBU is a network of regional small business organizations that represents the concerns of small business before lawmakers. SBU works regularly with congressional and executive branch officials in Washington and elsewhere. SBU offers no direct services to small businesses in particular; rather, it is a networking organization. Direct services are offered by member organizations. Member organizations might offer publications that provide key regional information. Here is a listing of these organizations:

SMALLER BUSINESS ASSOCIATION
  OF NEW ENGLAND
69 Hickory Drive
Waltham, MA 02254
(617) 890-9070

SMALLER MANUFACTURERS'
   COUNCIL*
1400 S. Braddock Avenue
Pittsburgh, PA 15218
(412) 371-1500

*Serves western Pennsylvania, eastern Ohio, and northern West Virginia.

INDEPENDENT BUSINESS
   ASSOCIATION OF WISCONSIN
3 S. Pinckney Street, Suite 26
Madison, WI 53703
(608) 251-5546

COUNCIL OF SMALLER ENTERPRISE*
200 Tower City
50 Public Square
Cleveland, OH 44113-2291
(216) 621-3300

*Serves Greater Cleveland and surrounding region.

SMALL BUSINESS
   ASSOCIATION OF MICHIGAN
P.O. Box 16158
Lansing, MI 48901
(517) 482-8788

INDEPENDENT BUSINESS
   ASSOCIATION OF ILLINOIS
680 N. Lake Shore Drive, #925
Niles, IL 60611
(312) 333-0067

OHIO SMALL BUSINESS COUNCIL
Ohio Chamber of Commerce
35 E. Gay Street
Columbus, OH 43215
(614) 228-4201

Industry support groups

The following industry-based associations also provide support services to member firms. For a more complete list, consult the NTPA Directory (see Appendix C).

Textile Mill Products

INDUSTRIAL FABRICS ASSOCIATION
  INTERNATIONAL
345 Cedar Building, Suite 800
St. Paul, MN 55101
(612) 222-8215

Lumber and Wood Products

INTERNATIONAL WOODWORKERS
  OF AMERICA
25 Cornell Avenue
Gladstone, OR 97027
(503) 656-1475

Chemical and Allied Products

CHEMICAL MANUFACTURERS
  ASSOCIATION
2501 M Street, NW
Washington, DC 20037
(202) 887-1100

Machinery, Except Electrical

FARM EQUIPMENT
  MANUFACTURERS ASSOCIATION
243 North Lindberg Boulevard
St. Louis, MO 63141
(314) 991-0702

NATIONAL TOOLING AND
  MACHINING ASSOCIATION
9300 Livingston Road
Fort Washington, MD 20744
(301) 248-6200

ASSOCIATION FOR
  MANUFACTURING TECHNOLOGY
7901 Westpark Drive
McLean, VA 22102
(703) 893-2900

Electric and Electronic Equipment

MOTOR AND EQUIPMENT
  MANUFACTURERS ASSOCIATION
P.O. Box 1638
Englewood Cliffs, NJ 07632
(201) 569-8500

NATIONAL ELECTRICAL
  MANUFACTURERS ASSOCIATION
2101 L Street, NW, #300
Washington, DC 20037
(202) 457-8400

ELECTRONIC INDUSTRIES
  ASSOCIATION
1722 Eye Street, NW
Washington, DC 20006
(202) 457-4900

Instruments and Related Products

SCIENTIFIC APPARATUS
  MAKERS ASSOCIATION
1101 16th Street, NW, Suite 300
Washington, DC 20036
(202) 223-1360

MANUFACTURERS AGENTS
  NATIONAL ASSOCIATION
P.O. Box 3467
Laguna Hills, CA 92654
(714) 859-4040

Wholesale Trade—Durable Goods

AUTOMOTIVE SERVICE
  INDUSTRY ASSOCIATION
444 North Michigan Avenue
Chicago, IL 60611
(312) 836-1300

INTERNATIONAL
  COMMUNICATIONS INDUSTRY
  ASSOCIATION
3150 Spring Street
Fairfax, VA 22031
(703) 273-7200

NATIONAL HARDWOOD
  LUMBER ASSOCIATION
Box 34518
Memphis, TN 38184-0518
(901) 377-1818

NATIONAL TIRE DEALERS AND
  RETREADERS ASSOCIATION,
  INCORPORATED
1250 Eye Street, NW, Suite 400
Washington, DC 20005
(202) 789-2300

Construction

ASSOCIATION GENERAL
  CONTRACTORS OF AMERICA
1957 E Street, N.W.
Washington, DC 20006
(202) 393-2040

ASSOCIATED BUILDERS
  AND CONTRACTORS, INC.
729 15th Street, N.W.
Washington, DC 20005
(202) 637-8800

Special Trade Contractors

AIR CONDITIONING
  CONTRACTORS OF AMERICA
1513 16th Street, NW
Washington, DC 20036
(202) 483-9370

AMERICAN SOCIETY OF
  PLUMBING ENGINEERS
3617 Thousand Oaks Blvd.
Westlake, CA 91362
(808) 495-7120

NATIONAL ELECTRICAL
  CONTRACTORS ASSOCIATION
7315 Wisconsin Avenue
Washington, DC 20814
(202) 657-3110

NATIONAL INSULATION
  CONTRACTORS ASSOCIATION
99 Canal Center Plaza, #222
Alexandria, VA 22314
(703) 683-6422

Index

Other Bestsellers of Related Interest

THE SMALL BUSINESS TAX ADVISOR:
Understanding The New Tax Law
—Cliff Roberson, LLM, Ph.D

The most extensive changes ever in the history of American tax laws were made in 1986. And to help you better understand these changes, Cliff Roberson has compiled the information every small business operator, corporate officer, director, or stockholder needs to know into a manageable and readily understandable new sourcebook. 176 pages. Book No. 30024, $12.95 paperback only

THE PERSONAL TAX ADVISOR: Understanding the New Tax Law—Cliff Roberson, LLM, Ph.D

How will the new tax law affect your tax return this filing season? Any reform is certain to mean a change in the way your taxes are prepared. But you don't have to be an accountant or a lawyer to understand the new tax laws . . . use this easy-to-read guide and learn how to reduce your income taxes under the new federal rules! 176 pages. Book No. 30134, $10.95 paperback only

FIGHT THE IRS AND WIN: A Self-Defense Guide for Taxpayers—Cliff Roberson

With this practical guide you can obtain the best results possible—protect your individual and property rights—in any dispute with the IRS. The outstanding feature of this book is that it takes complicated IRS operations and provides the average taxpayer with advice on how to protect himself in IRS controversies. It is the taxpayer's self-defense book. 224 pages. Book No. 30021, $12.95 paperback only

AVOIDING PROBATE: Tamper-Proof
Estate Planning—Cliff Roberson

Discover how to hand down everything you own to anyone you choose without interference from courts, creditors, relatives, or the IRS. In this easy-to-read planning guide, attorney Cliff Roberson shows how you can avoid the horrors of probate court. Sample wills and trust agreements and checklists in every chapter make planning each step easy. *Avoiding Probate* covers: living trusts, life insurance, specific property, wills, family businesses, valuing your estate, estate taxes, and more. 263 pages. Book No. 30074, $14.95 paperback, $29.95 hardcover

GETTING OUT: A Step-by-Step Guide to Selling a Business or Professional Practice
—Lawrence W. Tuller

A management consultant and former business owner, the author brings 25 years of buyout and acquisition experience to bear on the problems of establishing a "getting-out" position. He offers a complete and authoritative treatment of the subject for owners of any size business—as well as doctors, lawyers, accountants, and other professionals in private practice. 320 pages, 30 illustrations. Book No. 30063, $24.95 hardcover only

GOING PUBLIC: How to Make Your Initial Stock Offering Successful—Martin Weiss

This book contains the essential information business owners need to prepare for the problems, pressures and dangers of offering public stock. *Going Public* is a concise and extremely well-written overview of the process. Using the businessman's perspective, this guide covers: factors that affect the stock offering, finding a proficient underwriter, pricing the stock, dilution of earnings, and more. 168 pages, 47 illustrations. Book No. 30012, $12.95 paperback, $19.95 hardcover

GREAT AD!: Low-Cost, Do-It-Yourself Advertising for Your Small Business—Carol Wilkie Wallace

If you have big plans but a small budget, this book will help you to produce an effective, professional and economical advertising campaign. It takes a hands-on approach and walks you step-by-step through research, media planning, and creative strategy. *Great Ad!* Helps you research the competition, assess your business image, analyze the market, target your audience, schedule sales, and develop a media calendar. You also get hints on sources for artwork and music, and methods for effective copy. 352 pages, 36 illustrations. Book No. 3467, $19.95 paperback, $32.95 hardcover

FORMING CORPORATIONS AND
PARTNERSHIPS—John C. Howell

If you're considering offering a service out of your home, buying a franchise, incorporating your present business, or starting a business venture of any type you need this time- and money-saving guide. It explains in detail the process of creating a corporation, gives information on franchising, the laws of partnership, and more. 192 pages. Book No. 30143, $10.95 paperback only

UNDERSTANDING WALL STREET—2nd Edition
—Jeffery B. Little and Lucien Rhodes
*"An excellent introduction to stock market intrica-
cies"* **American Library Association Booklist**
   This bestselling guide to understanding and invest-
ing on Wall Street has been completely updated to reflect
the most current developments in the stock market. The
substantial growth of mutual funds, the emergence of
index options, the sweeping new tax bill, and how to
keep making money after the market reaches record
highs and lows are a few of the things explained in this
long awaited revision. 240 pages, 18 illustrations. Book
No. 30020, $9.95 paperback, $19.95 hardcover

**INSTANT LEGAL FORMS: Ready-to-Use
Documents for Almost Any Occasion**—Ralph E. Troisi
   By following the clear instructions provided in this
book, you can write your own will, lend or borrow
money or personal property, buy or sell a car, rent out a
house or apartment, check your credit, hire contractors,
and grant power of attorney—all without the expense or
complication of a lawyer. Author-attorney Ralph E.
Troisi supplies ready-to-use forms and step-by-step
guidance in filling them out and modifying them to meet
your specific needs. 224 pages, Illustrated. Book No.
30028, $15.95 paperback only

Prices Subject to Change Without Notice.

Look for These and Other TAB Books at Your Local Bookstore

To Order Call Toll Free 1-800-822-8158
(in PA, AK, and Canada call 717-794-2191)

or write to TAB BOOKS, Blue Ridge Summit, PA 17294-0840.

Title	Product No.	Quantity	Price

☐ Check or money order made payable to TAB BOOKS

Charge my ☐ VISA ☐ MasterCard ☐ American Express

Acct. No. _____ Exp. _____

Signature: _____

Name: _____

Address: _____

City: _____

State: _____ Zip: _____

Subtotal $ _____

Postage and Handling
($3.00 in U.S., $5.00 outside U.S.) $ _____

Add applicable state and local
sales tax $ _____

TOTAL $ _____

TAB BOOKS catalog free with purchase; otherwise send $1.00 in check
or money order and receive $1.00 credit on your next purchase.

Orders outside U.S. must pay with international money order in U.S. dollars.

**TAB Guarantee: If for any reason you are not satisfied with the book(s)
you order, simply return it (them) within 15 days and receive a full
refund.** **BC**